D0903033

Alchemy:
The Great Work

Alchemy:
The Great Work

Cherry Gilchrist

With a foreword by MARK BOOTH

A history and evaluation of the
Western Hermetic Tradition

WEISERBOOKS
San Francisco, CA / Newburyport, MA

This edition first published in 2015 by Weiser Books,
an imprint of Red Wheel/Weiser, LLC
With offices at:
665 Third Street, Suite 400
San Francisco, CA 94107
www.redwheelweiser.com

ISBN: 978-1-57863-585-6

Library of Congress Cataloging-in-Publication Data available upon request

Cover design by Graham Lester
Text design by Jane Hagaman

Printed in the United States of America
EBM
10 9 8 7 6 5 4 3 2 1

CONTENTS

FOREWORD

Few subjects have so intrigued and fascinated humankind down the
ages as alchemy—curious when you consider just how abstruse almost
all alchemical texts are. I have spent many hours reading these texts,
from Elias Ashmole's *Theatrum Chemicum Britannicum* to Fulcanelli's *Mysteres des Cathedrales*. I've travelled, for example, to the alchemist's house at Dampierre sur Boutonne that Fulcanelli described in
Dwellings of the Philosophers. I have debated alchemy on the banks of the
Nile with Robert Temple and Michael Baigent and tried to quiz someone—David Ovason—who claimed to have known practising alchemists.
Occasionally it all seems to be about to click into place and I've believed
myself on the point of cracking the code—but then it all goes hazy again.

So I am very glad that Cherry Gilchrist's great book *Alchemy: The
Great Work* is being brought back into print. I hadn't read it before I was
asked to write this foreword, but I'm very glad to have done so now. It is
packed with strange stories and shiny nuggets of information previously
unknown to me, references to 'the three *hun* souls and the seven *pho* souls
within one's body', the importance of 40, the number of the planet Venus
in the alchemical process if you are to see 'Venus unveiled', *The Hunting of
the Green Lion*, the French twentieth century alchemist Armand Barbault,
and the Rosicrucian sisterhood based in America and called The Woman
in the Wilderness.

There are some wonderful, tantalizing quotes, including from John of
Rupesciasa in the fourteenth century. He asserts that alchemy is 'the secret
of the mastery of fixing the sun in our own sky, so that it shines therein
and sheds light and principle of light on our bodies.' Could he be alluding
to what are called the chakras in Hindu tradition?

I was especially pleased to learn more about the role of women in
alchemy, including the wife of the famous alchemist Helvetius. She came
to him in the middle of the night 'soliciting and vexing me to make experiment of that little spark.' Why is it that alchemical texts sometimes sound
like sex manuals? Is there perhaps a parallel with any kind of tantric practice, sexual or otherwise?

Alchemy: The Great Work is erudite but reads very clearly. It covers all
the major manifestations of alchemy down through the ages from ancient
Egypt and China through its great flourishing in Alexandria, the legends

and manuals that emerged in the Middle Ages and Renaissance Europe, down to its late flourishing in the twentieth century, both in its chemical applications and as a form of therapy developed in the first instance by Carl Gustav Jung.

But what I admire about it most is how enlightening and enlivening it is. Cherry Gilchrist doesn't just tell you stuff, she sets you thinking. Alchemical ways of thinking and imagery will start making new patterns in your mind as you read it.

She shows that the people who try to insist that alchemy is all about manufacturing gold—with the strong implication that it is probably fraudulent or deluded—are completely wrong. Equally wrong, though, are the people who claim it has only ever been a form of spiritual exercise. Alchemy has embraced both. Indeed Cherry Gilchrist shows how alchemy has morphed down the ages in a way I've seen laid down before, and she also shows how alchemy and alchemical thought have informed chemistry, spiritual practice, the search for an elixir of youth, medicine, psychology, magic, and great art and writing, such as Shakespeare's and Donne's.

What I draw from all this is that alchemy is a Theory of Everything—but from a very particular point of view. It is a point of view diametrically opposed to that of the materialist physicists, for example 'string theorists,' who think they are on the very brink of devising a theory of everything that will explain away all outstanding mysteries and in the process do away with all need for religion or spirituality.

This alchemical point of view is what we might call Mind-Before-Matter—essentially the religious or spiritual view of life. Unlike modern materialist science, which asserts that consciousness is an accident of matter that arose quite late on in creation, this other view asserts that a great cosmic mind existed before matter and precipitated matter, bringing it into existence. As well as Mind-Before-Matter is also Mind-Over-Matter, asserting that the great cosmic mind controls the movement of matter in the cosmos.

A part of this religious view is that we humans, insofar as we too are made of mind—perhaps even carrying within us a small portion of this cosmic mind—also have the power to move matter *just by thinking about it*. Prayer is just one of the ways that religious or spiritual people can use mind to move matter. Other more alchemically tinged methods include the Christian Mass and also ceremonial magic.

It is perhaps not surprising that alchemy has informed the work of Shakespeare, Donne, and Jung. What is more surprising—not at all what you might expect—is that great advances in science seem to have been made by applying the alchemical theory of everything to the material world. Cherry Gilchrist shows how, for example, Paracelsus, application of alchemical theory to the peasants' remedies he collected and collated, and that in this way his search for the *arcanum* gave rise to modern medicine's drive to isolate the active ingredient in a substance through chemical processes.

Similarly, modern chemistry took from alchemy the principle of careful observation, and it was Newton's applying of alchemical theory to his observation of the behaviour of matter that led him to his revolutionary theories.

Of course this is not the history of science we have been taught! But if these ancient ways of thinking have proved useful, if they yield useful results and applications, testable ones at that, then might they be right?

I believe that this is a propitious time to take a fresh look at alchemy, and I recommend Cherry Gilchrist's *Alchemy: The Great Work* as a very wise, illuminating, and eminently readable place to start.

Mark Booth

WHAT IS ALCHEMY?

Alchemy is the art of transformation. The work of the alchemist is to bring about succeeding changes in the material he operates on, transforming it from a gross, unrefined state to a perfect and purified form. To turn base metals into gold is the simplest expression of this aim, and at the physical level this involves chemical operations performed with laboratory equipment. However, this is only one dimension of alchemy, since the 'base material' worked upon and the 'gold' produced may also be understood as man himself in his quest to perfect his own nature. Mainstream alchemy is a discipline involving physical, psychological, and spiritual work, and if any one of these elements is taken out of context and said to represent the alchemical tradition, then the wholeness and true quality of alchemy are lost.

For several reasons, it is not an easy tradition to understand. Firstly, the chief medium of alchemical expression is through the use of mythological symbols, which are the perfect means of conveying information that can be interpreted at both a material and a spiritual level, but which defy a single and precise definition. (They present similar problems to dreams, which can be interpreted successfully in several different ways.)

Secondly, alchemy's claims to produce extraordinary results in the physical world are hard to assess objectively. By the laws of science as normally understood today, it is not possible to convert other metals into gold, except by nuclear fission. But since alchemy encompasses mental as well as physical participation, it inevitably goes beyond the realms of material science in its scope and may be able to produce effects on the physical level that cannot be accounted for by normal chemistry. Additionally, as we shall see, the gold produced is usually said to be quite different from ordinary gold.

Thirdly, alchemy has a history stretching back for at least two thousand years and has been practised in Eastern, Arabic, and Western societies. It would be surprising indeed if it showed a uniform tradition of practice. Like any study, it has attracted many types of people with widely differing motivations. There have always been alchemists who were out-and-out materialists, greedy to try and make themselves rich by mastering the secret of creating gold. Some were merely gullible, others fraudulent, performing fake transmutations and getting their gold from the pockets of their spectators and prospective pupils rather than through any success in the laboratory. Even among the sincere and dedicated alchemists, the emphasis of approach could be very different. Some were interested more in the chemical techniques of alchemy, others in the philosophical aspects. Some saw alchemy as a path to the true meaning of Christianity, while others saw in it possibilities for producing subtle and potent medicines.

The knowledge and aim that each practitioner brought to alchemy coloured his attitude to it, and to some extent defined his mode of operation. There are certain key symbols and processes in alchemy, but no two descriptions of it are identical, which has caused many a headache for those who try and trace its history and significance. Writers on alchemy, like the alchemists themselves, define the tradition from their own viewpoint and inclinations. This is inevitable: there is no such thing as an 'objective' interpretation of alchemy. This should not pose a problem, provided that the reader realizes that a scientific, psychological, or spiritual training will undoubtedly create a different emphasis in a study of alchemy, since alchemy contains all these dimensions. Few of us are likely to be equally skilled and knowledgeable on all three levels, and our personal expertise and preference will determine our approach to alchemy and our insights into its operation. Taken at its most simple level, this means that a scientist will find alchemy of interest as a form of early chemistry, the psychologist will see it as a way of mapping the human psyche through symbolic descriptions, and the mystic will interpret it as a quest for divine knowledge.

Most investigators of alchemy have produced fresh and interesting insights and interpretations, but it is worth remembering that every writer has limitations, leading us to a new and exciting viewpoint for the alchemical landscape, perhaps, but often ignoring or dismissing certain key features of alchemy. C. G. Jung, the psychologist who did so much to bring the effectiveness of alchemical imagery to our attention, chose to reject the physical side of alchemy entirely. He admitted that alchemists did work in their laboratories, but stated dogmatically that 'the process never led to the desired goal' and was pursued by the alchemist only because 'there was nothing at the time to convince [him] of the senselessness of his operations.' Similarly, Lynn Thorndike, an able and meticulous historian who brought to light much fascinating material on alchemy, could not abide the use of symbol and myth in the alchemical texts, complaining that 'these allegories of the alchemists are insufferably tedious reading.'

Alchemy demands to be taken seriously; it has been practised by men of distinction in the fields of philosophy, science, medicine, and divinity who were inspired by its aims and who dedicated much time and material resources to its pursuit. In this book, I have attempted to give the tradition the respect that I feel is due to it, but at the same time to highlight some of the problems of interpretation, inviting the reader to consider their implications rather than offering simple solutions that would not do justice to the questions raised. I am not a scientist; my own interest lies chiefly in the symbolical and spiritual areas of alchemy, and these receive more attention in this book than do the chemical realities of the laboratory. However, there are several good books that trace the scientific aspect of alchemy in greater detail, and the reader will find suggestions in the select bibliography (p. 143) for further reading.

The Name Alchemy

The immediate derivation of the word alchemy is from the Arabic *al kimia*. *Al* means 'the,' —but the meaning of the second half of the word is not at all clear. One popular idea is that it is associated with the Egyptian word *chem*, signifying 'black' and relating to the description of Egypt as 'The Land of the Black Soil.' This would then define alchemy as 'The Egyptian Art' or 'The Black Art.' Some scholars, though, consider it more likely that the word is derived from *chyma*, a Greek word relating to the casting or fusing of metal. This in turn appears to come from *cheein*, meaning 'to pour out'; *cheein* has other variants, such as *chymos*, 'plant juice,' and *chylos*, a similar word but with the added association of 'taste.' It is possible that in the early days of alchemy the working of metals and the extraction of juices from plants were closely linked.*

The Time-Span of Alchemy

The text of this book will follow, broadly speaking, the chronological development of alchemy, but it will be useful here to look briefly at the timescale and geography involved. The origins of alchemy cannot be precisely dated, but it emerged as an art in its own right during the last two or three centuries BC, both in the Far East (especially in China), and in

---

* Readers who would like to investigate the etymology further are advised to read Chapter 4 of *The Origins of Alchemy in Graeco-Roman Egypt* by Jack Lindsay, which is entirely devoted to this topic.

Western civilization. In the West it centred on the Alexandrian culture, drawing together aspects of both the Egyptian and the classical Greek worlds. The alchemy of the East had a preoccupation with creating an elixir of longevity, while that of the Graeco-Egyptian culture dealt chiefly with metals and minerals. Both aspired to knowledge of creation and universal order; both schools fell into a decline by the fifth and sixth centuries AD. However, while the Eastern tradition carried on (with cyclical ups and downs) right through the succeeding centuries, the Western school shifted location into the Arabic world, where it was enthusiastically practised and developed until Europeans climbed back out of the 'Dark Ages' and began to take an interest in the traditions of learning that the Arabs had preserved. From the twelfth century onwards, most European countries adopted alchemy as a study in its own right. Its reputation fluctuated. Sometimes it was considered to be a most elevated study, sometimes it was looked upon as the profession of rogues and knaves. Some kings and emperors were enthusiastic alchemists themselves, while others brought out statutes forbidding its practice. Alchemy was always an emotive topic, and throughout its history there has gone up a continual lament from its practitioners that they are misunderstood by an ignorant public.

During the sixteenth and seventeenth centuries, there was an eagerness among men of learning to gather the strands of study together, to compare and synthesize the arts, sciences, and systems of occult and divine knowledge. Triggered by the Renaissance ideal, and perpetuated by such bodies as the Rosicrucian school of philosophy, this movement gained momentum and resulted in alchemy being brought out more into the open and set alongside other disciplines. Until then, it had been treated as a secret, private study, whose knowledge was to be passed on only directly by word of mouth or through the ambiguity of symbol and allegory. As it was discussed and practised more freely, so its quality changed. Many of the principles, symbols, and ideas of alchemy were incorporated into the other branches of learning, such as medicine and physics, and alchemy itself receded from the public eye and was indeed thought extinct by many.

However, until the present day it has been practised quietly by a few adherents, and now the tradition is once more arousing interest. Its imagery has shown its enduring value by finding a place in modem psychology, and the practice of a discipline that involves both scientific and psychic skills is again showing its appeal. Alchemy has reached a point of reappraisal and, reformulated, it may once again be considered a serious subject for study.

The Aim of Alchemy

Alchemists have always looked upon their work as a way of life, insisting that it needs dedication and sincerity of intention if it is to produce any results. They speak of it in such terms as 'our sacred philosophy,' the 'work of wisdom,' the 'Great Work,' and the 'divine activity.' The term 'our' is used freely in alchemical texts ('our gold,' 'our mercury,' 'our work,' etc.), implying not possessiveness, but a special alchemical form of substances and secret methods of preparation that were understood by the true practitioners but not by outsiders. It was a way of distinguishing alchemy from ordinary pharmacy and metalworking, but it also had the effect of suggesting the existence of an exclusive band of initiates who had access to knowledge denied to ordinary mortals. While this made it clear that alchemy was more than a material craft, it also helped to induce the envy and ridicule that has dogged alchemists throughout the centuries—emotions naturally aroused when it is made plain that there is a secret that one is not allowed to know!

The fundamental aim of alchemy was the production of the *Philosopher's Stone,* also known as the *Elixir,* or *Tincture.* The proof of the Stone was that it would turn a base metal into gold. Thus the transmutation into gold was seen as a mark of success, but the power lay in the Stone itself, which was the transmuting agent. It is easy for these two elements to become confused in the interpretation of alchemy, and even the alchemical texts themselves are not always clear on this point. The Stone is usually said to have something of the nature of gold in itself; it is the active element that was thought to accelerate the natural process of perfection in material. (Gold, as we shall see, was said to grow from base metals within the earth, and alchemical transmutation was therefore a speeded-up process of evolution.) The gold it could produce, however, was frequently said to be quite different from ordinary gold, being a more perfect form, and was accordingly called by such terms as 'our gold,' 'exalted gold,' or 'the gold of the Sages.'

The Stone was not usually described as stonelike in substance, but more often as a powder or wax that could also be rendered into a liquid form, which corresponds better with the appellations of Tincture and Elixir. Its power was not only as an agent of metallic transformation, but as the very secret of transformation itself, in both the physical and the spiritual realms:

The Philosopher's Stone is called the most ancient, secret or unknown, naturally incomprehensible, heavenly, blessed sacred Stone of the Sages. It is described as being true, more certain than certainty itself, the arcanum of all arcana—the Divine virtue and efficacy, which is hidden from the foolish, the aim and end of all things under heaven, the wonderful epilogue of conclusion of all the labours of the Sages—the perfect essence of all the elements, the indestructible body which no element can injure, the quintessence; the double and living mercury which has in itself the heavenly spirit—the cure for all unsound and imperfect metals—the everlasting light—the panacea for all diseases—the glorious Phoenix—the most precious of all treasures—the chief good of Nature.[1]

The Stone was seen as the key to knowledge, which only a wise man can use responsibly:

If an athlete know not the use of his sword, he might as well be without it; and if another warrior that is skilled in the use of that weapon come against him, the first is likely to fare badly. For he that has knowledge and experience on his side, must carry off the victory.

In the same way, he that possesses this tincture, by the grace of Almighty God, and is unacquainted with its uses, might as well not have it at all . . . [But] whoever uses this as a medium shall find whither the vestibules of the palace lead, and there is nothing comparable to the subtlety thereof. He shall possess all in all performing all things whatsoever which are possible under the sun.[2]

It was made very plain that alchemy was just as much to do with self-mastery as with mastery of the physical laws of Nature, and that neither could be achieved without patience, observation, and devotion. Sometimes the aspect of personal transformation was stated very clearly, as by John of Rupescisia, who wrote in the fourteenth century that alchemy is 'the secret of the mastery of fixing the sun in our own sky, so that it shines therein and sheds light and the principle of light upon our bodies.'

The Alchemical Process

The art of the alchemist, then, is to activate a process that will transform a first substance, or *prima materia*, into the Philosopher's Stone. The process is of tremendous importance and carries no guarantee of success, since the attitude of the alchemist, the timing of events, and the materials and equipment used must all harmonize and combine in exactly the right way. Often alchemists spent several decades in their search and attributed their ultimate success to outside aid—either divine or human—rather than to mechanical repetition and variation in their technique. After looking through various alchemical texts, one is left with the impression that there was in fact no one precise formula, which, if followed to the letter, would bring about the desired end. There are only principles of operation that the alchemist must apply with a high level of awareness and judgement. Indeed, the process, with all its potential setbacks and problems, is itself the education of the alchemist, and until he has developed his own skills and insights through this, he cannot perfect the Work.

The alchemist is described as the artist who, through his operations, brings Nature to perfection. But the process is also like the unfolding of the Creation of the world, to which the alchemist is a witness as he watches the changes that take place within the vessel. The vessel is a universe in miniature, a crystalline sphere through which he is privileged to see the original drama of transformation:

> Neither be anxious to ask whether I actually possess this precious treasure. Ask rather whether I have seen how the world was created; whether I am acquainted with the nature of the Egyptian darkness, what is the cause of the rainbow; what will be the appearance of the glorified bodies at the general resurrection . . .[3]

The process itself consists of taking the primal material and subjecting it to chemical treatment, chiefly by heat and distillation, until it finally—perhaps only after years—comes to perfection. In terms of physical operation, alchemy differs from chemistry in its insistence on two factors: firstly, the timing of operations to accord with appropriate astrological configurations; and secondly, the repetition of certain stages of the process to an extraordinary extent (such as distilling several hundred times). Some writers on alchemy, emphasizing its value as a spiritual discipline, have belittled the importance of its physical operations, but there is no doubt that the processing of physical substances, even though this was carried out in a different manner to that of modern chemistry, was equally important in the art. Archibald Cockren, a twentieth-century alchemist, explains the necessity of this:

That this preparation is a physical process carried out in a laboratory with water, retorts, sand-bath, and furnaces, there is no doubt.
That alchemy is purely a psychic and spiritual science has no basis
in fact. A science to be a science must be capable of manifestation
on every plane of consciousness; in other words it must be capable of demonstrating the axiom 'as above, so below.' Alchemy can
withstand this test, for it is, physically, spiritually, and psychically, a
science manifesting throughout all form and all life.[4]

As I have implied, one can talk about the different stages of the process
only in general terms, since descriptions of it vary. Most texts also indicate
that they are holding back a particular secret, which is essential for the
completion of the operation. Often this relates to the primal material, the
substance needed to start the process, whose composition is only hinted
at. We will look at this fascinating mystery later, but for the moment, it is
enough to say that the first material of alchemy is frequently described as
something of metallic origin, yet not outwardly resembling a metal, a base
substance known to all yet recognized only by the wise. If this substance
is treated correctly, it needs the addition of nothing else to become the
Philosopher's Stone, for it has within its essence the potential power of the
stone, and it is the alchemist's task to bring this potential to realization:

> For there is only *one* substance,
> In which all the rest is hidden;
> Therefore, keep a good heart.
> Coction, time, and patience are what you need;
> If you would enjoy the precious reward,
> You must cheerfully give both time and labour.
> For you must subject to gentle coction the seeds and the metals,
> Day by day, during several weeks;
> Thus in this one vile thing
> You will discover and bring to perfection the whole work of
>   Philosophy. [5]

The outward form of the primal material must be destroyed, by fire or
special acidic preparations. Sometimes this is described as setting the two
dragons at war with one another. Thus the male and female principles of
the matter are released and can be reunited in a stage often depicted as
the marriage of the King and Queen. Further treatment of the substance

in the vessel by heat leads to its 'death,' a moment known as the *nigredo*, or 'blackening.' But the 'soul' of the matter still lingers in the hermetically sealed vessel and may be induced to condense in liquid form and return to the body once more. This is the resurrection, which may be heralded by a glorious show of iridescent colours known as 'The Peacock's Tail.' The child of the union must be gently nurtured, usually by adding a liquid that may have been extracted from the vessel at an earlier stage. With the right food and heat, it grows until it 'whitens,' indicating that the Elixir is perfected in its first degree. The White Stone, as it is known, is said to be capable of transmuting metals into silver. It is the female tincture, equated with the moon. To gain the gold-giving tincture, the sun, further treatment is necessary until the Elixir reddens. Then it is the Red Rose, grown from the White Rose, the ultimate goal of the process.

As can be seen, alchemy describes its operations in vividly symbolic statements. Terms such as birth, death, and resurrection are not used as mere associations but as indications of real states through which the matter must pass. The use of beasts, birds, and archetypal human figures who fight, marry, and copulate expresses the dynamic energies of the process. The different colours of each stage are the heraldic colours of transformation, announcing the dawning of a new 'day' in the creation.

This is the fundamental structure of the alchemical process, but many variants will be discovered and the order of the stages may differ slightly. The definition of what constitutes a stage in the process is very loose, and authors may claim a different number of essential operations. Usually the number involved is one that is symbolically satisfying, such as seven, ten, or twelve—for instance, the seven can be likened to the sequence of the seven days of creation, the twelve to the number of the zodiacal signs. We shall be looking at individual symbols and stages in more detail later. Throughout the book, quotations will be given from different alchemical texts, enabling the reader to gain an idea of the quality of description of the alchemical process.

Alchemical Texts

Alchemical texts are noted for their enigmatic utterances, obscurity, and maddening references to unrevealable secrets. Yet they are immensely stimulating, both to the imagination and the intellect, even though there is little consistency of exposition between one text and another, only certain key themes and symbols that recur regularly but not invariably.

One reason for this is that the tradition of alchemy has always been at least half-hidden from public view, and that the texts have been deliberately constructed to conceal certain alchemical directions from the reader. Another reason is that, over the centuries, different schools of alchemy have grown up, each with its own particular code of imagery and philosophical framework. There are obvious differences, for instance, between a Chinese Taoist alchemist and an English Christian alchemist, since the alchemy in question is coloured by the religion and culture of the practitioner. Even within a narrower context, it is likely that different alchemical disciplines were operating: these could probably be defined more closely, but it would be a mammoth task, complicated by the fact that many texts were written anonymously or ascribed to illustrious figures such as Solomon or Isis in order to give them authority.

The reader of alchemical works soon learns to discern the general orientation of an alchemical author—whether he was interested in mystical Christian alchemy or in chemical advances, for instance. It is also possible for the reader to decide on the quality and depth of a piece of alchemical writing. Some texts are patently profound, philosophical, and lucid, while others are confused, disjointed, and superficial. Some plainly speak a measure of truth from a living tradition, whereas others are written from secondhand experience, or are synthesized in a misguided fashion from other sources. Such an approach may not find favour with scholars, but my view is that anyone interested in the living core of alchemy must find some personal way of penetrating the dense jungle of alchemical books, manuscripts, expositions, and illustrations. The alchemical tradition has gathered many great men to it along the way; it has also drawn to it many rogues and fools:

> All that call themselves alchemists are not therefore necessarily true possessors of the Stone. For, as in other branches of knowledge, there are found many different schools and sects, so all that are in search of this precious Tincture are called alchemists, without necessarily deserving the name.[6]

THE SEARCH FOR TRANSFORMATION

In this chapter we shall be looking at the origins of alchemy in the Western and Eastern traditions and seeing how classical theories of matter and natural law influenced the fundamental ideas of alchemy. Man's early interest in metalworking and in the properties of precious metals also helped to build the alchemical framework, but alchemy has always been distinguished from craft work in that it involves a quest for knowledge that encompasses the divine as well as the material realm, and, indeed, does not perceive a division between them.

Gold

Gold is the focal symbol of alchemy. It is the crowning glory of the Work, the most perfect of metals, and every alchemist has aimed to master the secret of its creation, whether he saw this as an end in itself or as an outward token of his success in perfecting the alchemical art of transformation. Gold is more than a metal—it is a principle; and thus while physical, metallic gold holds a central position in alchemy, yet we also meet with the ideas of exalted gold, vegetable gold, and spiritual gold. It will be helpful at this point to look at the history of man's use of gold and to consider some of its cultural and religious associations in order that we may understand why it was treated with such reverence in alchemy.

When we look at the properties of gold it becomes apparent that it is a very special metal. It is almost immune to the normal processes of decay. It does not rust or tarnish; a hoard of gold coins buried a thousand years ago will be as bright when they are dug up as when they were hidden. Fire will refine gold, but not destroy it or alter its basic nature. Its aesthetic properties have been described as 'a smooth, soft texture, a beauty of colour, and a capacity to shine steadily.'[1] For the metal worker, it has considerable attractions since it can, if necessary, be worked cold rather than in a heated state. It is soft, which means that though it cannot be used for making sharp or durable implements, it can be crafted into delicately tooled shapes and patterns; it can also be beaten out to an incredible thinness to form gold foil or leaf.

Gold is found in all the continents of the earth and has therefore been known to practically every human civilization. It is comparatively rare and is often found in association with granite. In earliest times, gold would have been collected from near the surface, and the discovery of nuggets lying in the earth under an uprooted tree, for instance, must have had a truly magical quality. Panning for gold—the separating out of grains of gold from deposits at the bottom of river beds—was another early technique. The natural weight of gold as an element is considerable, making it relatively easy to wash away the lighter accumulations of silt and grains of sand, leaving the gold behind. The first known examples of gold worked by man appear around the fourth millenium BC. In Egypt and Ur, gold was used for jewellery, vessels, ornaments, and the adornment of royal tombs. Today we tend to think of coinage as an ancient use for gold, but in fact gold was not used as a currency until about 400 BC. Egypt had a rich supply of gold, and gold production was a state-controlled operation. Accounts of conditions in the Egyptian mines paint a gruesome picture of forced labour by criminals and prisoners of war, who, irrespective of health or age, had to work long hours at cutting, sorting and grinding the rock.

From early times, gold was associated with royalty and divinity. The Egyptians called gold 'the flesh of the gods,' and in legend, when a king attained divinity, his limbs and features were often transformed into gold in the process. Gold was regarded as the king of metals; it was therefore also seen as the metal of kings and of the King of the Universe. The Egyptians and other ancient peoples saw attributes of divinity within gold— effulgence, purity, incorruptibility—and thus gold itself embodied the power of the divine and could confer especial blessings and gifts through its use. Golden vessels, for instance, were thought to transform the quality of the drink they contained. From this we can see that gold was made into beautiful jewellery and ornaments not merely for decorative purposes, but to act beneficially upon the wearer, as a talisman or token of connection with the deities.

Gold also had an early correspondence with the sun that still persists. With similarities of colour and radiance, it is easy to see why. Silver, always linked closely with gold in alchemy, is the second of the heavenly pair; gold and silver are seen as king and queen, brother and sister, sun and moon. In Egypt and in Tibetan culture, they are the heavenly eyes, and it is said that 'the right eye of the Supreme Being is the Sun and his left eye is the Moon.' Planets, sun, and moon have long been closely associated with metals, and an interaction was perceived between them, chiefly that of the planets affecting the formation of metals, which the alchemist drew on in his work.

Gold has been esteemed universally as a magical, influential, other-worldly metal. In European traditions, fairies and dwarves were thought to be in possession of fabulous amounts of gold and silver. Gold was often used to tempt a mortal to join a being from the world of faery. A hill king in a Swedish ballad woos an earthly maiden by promising: 'Thee will I give the ruddiest gold . . . And thy chests full of money as they can hold.' In a more sinister British ballad entitled 'The Demon Lover,' the evil enchanter persuades his former mistress to leave her husband and child and sail away with him in a ship whose mast is of 'shining gold.' As he draws her further and further into his power he casts 'a glamour o'er her face | And it shone like the brightest gold.'

Gold, therefore, was not merely a symbol of wealth but an attribution of fairyland itself. There, the roof is made 'o' the beaten gould,' the horses are shod with golden shoes, and the music comes from golden harps. Sometimes there is a golden bridge by which the spirits enter and leave their kingdom. Gold is associated with power, danger, enchantment, and transformation. In nearly all cultures in which it is esteemed, it has been seen as more than a mere metal, and it is this power in gold which the alchemists acknowledged and chose to represent the goal of their work.

The Metal Workers

The craft of metalwork helped to build a foundation for alchemy and had already been in existence long before alchemy itself first came to light around 200 BC. Alchemy was strongly influenced by Egyptian traditions, and Egypt had been a centre for metal workers who raised their craft to a high degree. They knew how to make alloys and how to tint metals; they could colour gold with varnishes and understood gold plating. Some of their art was directed towards satisfying the ever-present human need to obtain more for less, since there were recipes for debasing gold with other metals to increase its apparent weight, and even to make fake gold.

However, the craftsmen undoubtedly took a great pride in their work, and they guarded its secrets jealously. Mastery of gold, silver, bronze, and iron has been responsible for far-reaching changes in the history of man, and those who understood this took pains to keep the powerful knowledge to themselves and their appointed successors. Sherwood Taylor says:

> It is an undoubted fact that the winning and working of gold were in ancient Egypt the subject of a priestly craft centred upon the temple of the god Ptah at Memphis. The god was 'master of gold smelters and goldsmiths,' his temple the 'goldsmithy' and his priests were distinguished by such titles as 'Great Wielder of the Hammer,' 'He who knows the Secret of the Goldsmiths.'[2]

Such secrecy, of course, accords well with alchemical practice, and Egyptian metal craft may well be the root from which alchemy sprang. We have few details of how this craft was practised, but certain general principles are known from paintings or hieroglyphs of the time. The smelter's furnace, for instance, was built up high on three sides to intensify the heat when the metal was being refined, and a blowpipe was used to increase the height of the flames. The earliest alchemists would probably have been initiated into the art of metalwork, but exactly how and when the two arts began to take on a separate identity is not certain.

The First Alchemists in the West

We only know of the existence of alchemists if they chose to reveal their presence, and if their writings have survived them. Therefore, while the earliest alchemical texts we now have date from the third century BC, according to some authorities, we cannot tell how many practising alchemists there were before this date, or how strong the tradition was at its recorded inception, since there are very few texts available until we come to the fourth to seventh centuries AD, the period that marks the first flowering of alchemy in the West. Although the alchemists themselves have always claimed a venerable pedigree for their art, stretching back to Plato, Moses, and the god Hermes himself, this is no help in dating its origins, even though it lends a general confirmation to the notion that alchemy is older than its known history.

It is helpful to try and understand the attitude of the alchemists themselves, which was indeed the attitude of nearly all men of learning until the Renaissance. It maintained that in the past man was the master of all wisdom, and that his passage through time has been marked by a gradual forgetting of ancient secrets, which later generations try to recapture. A tradition like alchemy upheld the belief that its initiates had kept such secrets uncorrupted throughout the centuries, and that by entering into the alchemical discipline a person could, with the right guidance, come into the possession of this wisdom. It was then the alchemist's duty to preserve and guard this for suitable candidates of the next generation, making sure that it was kept from those who would pervert its course. Such an attitude may seem strange to us today, but in fact it is no more illogical than the contemporary view that one day in the future man will know, understand, and master all the laws of the natural world. Both views are idealized and unrealistic.

In the case of alchemy, therefore, it was common for authors to establish a worthy pedigree for their writings, by ascribing the teachings to earlier masters, or claiming direct descent from the original divine or mythical patrons of the art. It was an attempt to lend weight to their words, rather than to deceive. Nevertheless, this does not help the historian, and we find that the beginnings of alchemy are shrouded in obscurity. Going backwards in time, the trail of practitioners becomes thinner and thinner until it fades into a world of myth. It is affirmed, for instance, that the goddess Isis herself was an initiate, having wrested the secrets of the making of gold and silver from a reluctant angel, on condition that she passed on the knowledge to no one but her own son Horus.

Alchemy, then, is likely to have hidden roots in pre-Alexandrian Egypt, in the nation devoted to magical, ritual, and technological achievement. Although this cannot be proved conclusively, there are suggestions from the early alchemists that we know of which corroborate this. Zosimos, writing around AD 300, says:

> The whole of the kingdom of Egypt . . . depends on these two arts, that of seasonable things† and that of minerals. For that which is called the divine art, whether in its dogmatic and philosophic aspect or its phenomena in general, was given to the wardens for their support; and not only this art, but also those which are called the four liberal arts and the technical manipulations, for their creative capacity is the property of kings. So that, if the kings permitted it, one who had received the knowledge as an inheritance from his ancestors would interpret it, whether from oral tradition or from the inscribed columns. But he who had the knowledge of these things in full did not himself practise the Art, for he would have been punished. In the same way, under the Egyptian kings the workers of the chemical operations and those who had the knowledge of the procedure did

---

† Possibly astrology.

not work for themselves, but served the Egyptian kings, working to fill their treasuries. For they had special masters set over them and a strict supervision was kept, not only upon the chemical operations, but also upon the gold-mines. For if anyone in mining found any-thing, it was a law among the Egyptians that it should be handed in for entry in the public register.[3]

Zosimos is accurate in his description of the control over mining, which strengthens the possibility that he is speaking from genuine knowledge about the secrecy of early alchemy.

The first known and named alchemical text is probably that by **Bolos of Mendes**, who wrote a book entitled *Physika*. This dealt with a variety of alchemical and pseudo-alchemical crafts, such as the making of gold, silver, gems, and the production of purple dye. Bolos tried to ascribe his work to the philosopher Demokrites (Democritus), father of the atomic theory, who lived in the fifth century BC. It is possible that the writings of Bolos date to around 250 BC, but some authorities would regard them as products of the first or second century AD. Other early extant texts are known as the Leiden and Stockholm Papyri, but these, while going under the name of alchemy, seem to be merely collections of recipes for mak-ing false gold and silver and for tinting and alloying metals. One recipe begins: 'To give objects of copper the appearance of gold so that neither the feel nor rubbing on the touchstone will discover it . . .'

With these texts we move to the early years of the current era, and to the flourishing Alexandrian culture in which alchemy throve. Alexandria was founded as a city by the Emperor Alexander on the north coast of Egypt in the fourth century BC and soon became a centre of great influ-ence in the fields of philosophy, mathematics, astrology, science, medi-cine, and indeed every other branch of learning then practised. It was a city of mixed nationalities, containing Greek, Jewish, Egyptian, Per-sian, Syrian, and Christian inhabitants. When powerful cultures meet in peace or war, there is often a remarkable stimulation of ideas; the coming together of the European and Arabic cultures at the time of the Crusades can be cited as an example. In Alexandria this contact was affirmed and crystallized through the founding of schools of learning and the estab-lishment of the great Alexandrian library. Scholars travelled from far and wide to study the ancient and contemporary texts housed there, which represented the whole spectrum of knowledge of the classical and Egyp-tian civilizations. Had this library not been destroyed at a later date by the Arab invasion, our knowledge of the ancient world would be infinitely greater than it is.

Another notable name from this early period of Alexandrian alchemy is that of **Maria the Jewess**, who is quoted with respect by other alchemists of the time and who lived around AD 100. She seems to have been a practical and inventive lady who improved the alchemical apparatus of the day. The *bain-marie* is named after her—the warm water bath that allows gentle cooking and that is still used in modem kitchens. Certain other texts from the same period are ascribed to **Kleopatra**, and while most historians are inclined to regard this as an attempt to elevate the famous Queen Cleopatra to the status of an alchemical priestess, Jack Lindsay, on the other hand, considers that the works originate from the school of a different Kleopatra, a lady alchemist of the time whose teachings were perpetuated by her disciples. The writings in question are *The Dialogue of Kleopatra and the Philosophers* and *The Gold-Making of Kleopatra*. From the former comes a precise description of the alchemical process:

> Take from the four elements the arsenic which is highest and lowest, the white and the red, the male and the female in equal balance, so that they may be joined to one another. For just as the bird warms her eggs with her heat and brings them to their appointed term, so yourselves warm your composition and bring it to its appointed term. And when you've borne it out and caused it to drink of the divine Waters in the Sun and in heated places, cook it upon a gentle fire with the virginal milk, keeping it from the smoke. Then shut the ingredients up in Hades and stir carefully until the preparation becomes thicker and does not run from the fire. Then remove it from the fire; and when the soul and spirit are unified and become one, project upon the body of silver and you will have gold such as the treasuries of kings do not contain.[4]

One of the best known authors of the period is **Zosimos**, quoted earlier in the chapter, whose writings give us some fine examples of visionary alchemy, which will be considered in detail in the next chapter. Another well-known name is that of **Stephanos of Alexandria** (*fl.* seventh century AD), said to have found fame at the court of the Emperor Herakleios at Byzantium, a royal patron who took an interest in alchemy. The writings of Stephanos appeared towards the end of this first phase of alchemy and are more philosophical than practical. Already, in this early period, we find a mixture of texts, ranging from the most mundane recipes for tinting or dyeing, to exalted tracts of esoteric teaching. Alchemy was emerging into public awareness, and often its practitioners, as well as those outside the art, must have been confused as to what exactly constituted alchemy, especially if it had arisen in the first instance from the secret guilds of the dyers and metalworkers. Possibly any information relating to these crafts was hoarded and examined, and much may have been designated alchemy which in time was seen as peripheral.

Laboratory work was certainly prominent in early alchemy, and a good deal of information survives as to the type of equipment used. *Cupellation,* a technique already known in ancient Egypt, was used to refine metals. A cupel consisted of a crucible, made usually of bone ash, which was supported by its lips about the edge of a furnace. The metal to be refined was placed within it and it was subjected to intense heat, sometimes closed in a kiln for several days until the impurities were either driven off by the heat or absorbed into the crucible itself.

A special feature of alchemy was *distillation,* and it remained a technique unique to alchemy for many centuries (see p. 111). A *still,* or *alembic,* was used. The material to be heated would be placed at the bottom of the still; there was a cool section above to condense the vapour driven off by the heat, and some means of collecting the liquid thus distilled. Maria the Jewess, mentioned above for her prowess in designing more efficient apparatus, invented a new still which Zosimos describes:

> Make three tubes of ductile copper a little thicker than that of a pastry-cook's copper frying pan: their length should be about a cubit and a half. Make three such tubes and also make a wide tube of a handsbreadth width and an opening proportioned to that of the still head. The three tubes should have their openings adapted like a nail to the neck of a light receiver, so that they have the thumb-tube and the two finger-tubes joined laterally on either hand. Towards the bottom of the still-head are three holes adjusted to the tubes, and when these are fitted they are soldered in place, the one above receiving the vapour in a different fashion. Then setting the still-head upon the earthenware pan containing the sulphur, and luting the joints with flour paste, place at the ends of the tubes glass flasks, large and strong so that they may not break with the heat coming from the water in the middle.[5]

Although sulphur is mentioned here as the material to be distilled, it is quite possible that this did not refer to sulphur as we know it but to the Primal Material, the secret substance that is transformed into the gold-making tincture. Sulphur, mercury, and salt in alchemical terminology refer to the three qualities of matter—spirit, soul, and body respectively—and not to the common substances of these names. Sometimes one of these terms would be used to designate the first material of the operation.

Another invention of the time was the *kerotakis,* a piece of equipment that created vapours out of a substance, through the application of heat; the vapours would then affect a portion of metal placed in the top part of the apparatus. The result would frequently emerge as an alloy, but it is likely that the idea of imparting colour through the use of the kerotakis was also important, since the word carries the meaning of 'artist's palette.'

From the earliest days, colour changes have played a significant part in alchemy. Each stage of the process has been associated with a different colour, and a correct sequence of colour changes has always been considered of critical importance in ascertaining whether the work is proceeding along the right lines. To the alchemists, colour has always been much more than an outward quality of matter; colour is the *pneuma* or life spirit of a substance. Changes of colour are a visible sign that transformation is taking place within matter.

The Greek alchemists recognized four distinct stages of colour change in the process, a successive blackening, whitening, yellowing, and reddening of the material in the vessel. (Sometimes red and purple were used synonymously.) Black was equated with the death of matter, and white with its rebirth in a purified form. The exact meaning of the yellowing is not clear, and this stage was often omitted in later descriptions of alchemy; but the reddening was always seen as the final perfection of the matter that had been transformed from a gross state into the longed-for Stone or Tincture. Although it was considered that no stage had been successfully accomplished unless the appropriate colour was manifested, yet it should be noted that colour on its own did not necessarily denote success. Warning is given, for instance, of a premature reddening, which could occur through hasty and careless work and which must be corrected at once.

The key sequence of black, white, and red has remained throughout the history of alchemy, with occasional variations and additions. The most common addition is that of the iridescent stage known as the *Peacock's Tail,* the rainbow, or the starry sky, which usually occurs after the *nigredo,* or blackening. Colour is an intrinsic part of the alchemical drama; with a little imagination the reader can easily see how, after perhaps months of patient observation, the alchemist was affected profoundly by the appearance of a new and dazzling hue in the hermetic vessel.

Theories of Elements and Metals

There are four elements, and . . . each has at its center another element which makes it what it is. These are the four pillars of the world. They were in the beginning evolved and moulded out of chaos by the hand of the Creator; and it is their contrary action which keeps up the harmony and equilibrium of the mundane machinery; it is they, which through the virtue of celestial influences, produce all things above and beneath the earth.[6]

Michael Sendivogius, writing in the seventeenth century, is here describing a classical theory of the construction of matter that formed the basis of ideas on alchemical transformation from the early period until the eighteenth century. The four elements are earth, water, fire, and air, and were first mentioned by the Greek philosopher Empedocles, who flourished c. 450 BC. These were seen as combining in different proportions to form every substance in existence; in alchemy part of the task was to rearrange the composition of the elements and their relationship to one another in order to transform the substance itself.

Aristotle's exposition of the theory was formulated c. 350 BC and held sway in Europe until the new era of science dawned in the seventeenth century. He held that each element was composed of two qualities, there being four qualities in all—hot, dry, moist, and cold. The element of air was hot and moist; fire was hot and dry; earth dry and cold; and water cold and moist. By changing a quality of each element, transformation became possible: by driving out the moisture from air, for instance, fire would result since the pair of qualities would now be those of fire, which was hot and dry. This provided the alchemists with a theory of transformation.

The apparent simplicity of this system, however, is undermined by the alchemists' own descriptions of it, as we can see from the quotation above. They were quick to point out that true air, fire, water, and earth were not the common entities that we know. The 'common' elements were the visible or tangible qualities that came closest in character to the 'pure' elements. These pure elements were found only at the very heart of matter, and were seen more as forces, or agencies, rather than as detectable substances. They carried out the work of Nature by combining and recombining to create all the different types of matter on the earth. If matter changed its state, as it did in the alchemical vessel, then this signified that the proportions of elements forming the matter had been transformed and recombined. A change in the elemental state could not be brought about by mere physical force, such as by grinding or cutting. Usually it was thought to be produced only by the application of another elemental agent, that of fire or water especially.

Thus 'common' fire and water played a prominent part in alchemy, but frequently the alchemists sought to make the 'pure' forms, which they called by such names as 'our fire' and 'the sweet water,' the 'Pontic water' or 'the water of the wise.' These were the subject of lengthy preparation and were used for such purposes as the destruction of the original form of the Primal Material in order to liberate the elements within it, or for nourishing the material in the vessel when it had already undergone radical transformation.

Although modern nuclear theories of matter make no mention of earth, water, fire, and air, and although the definition of the word 'element' has changed completely, the classical theory of the elements espoused by the alchemists is nevertheless a view of the universe that can shed much light upon the qualities of matter. (The terms still hold good in astrology, where they are used to describe characteristics of the human personality.) All theories of the basic composition of matter are in time superceded, but each contains a certain understanding of the laws of nature, even if in an incomplete form. In the Greek theory of the elements as developed by the alchemists, earth represents the stabilizing, material principle of matter that adds weight and solidity; water is nourishing, pervasive, and dissolving; fire is quickening, illuminating, and heating; air is expansive and lightens the balance of the other three.

Gold was considered to contain the perfect balance of all four elements. Nature, it was said, operated a constant process of perfecting that which was originally gross or corrupt. Aristotle, once again, was responsible for first putting forward the theory that Nature 'grew' gold in the earth and that all metals, in due course, would grow to become gold. Metals themselves grew from seeds, which might not normally be recognized as being metallic in their primal state. Sometimes the alchemical quest for the Primal Material was described as a search for the right metallic seed, which the alchemist could nurture and grow into its perfect golden state. (There seem to have been two schools of thought operating here, since, as we have already seen, the commonly stated aim of the process was to produce the Stone that was a gold-creating agent, a catalyst to be used on base metals to turn them into gold. Both ideas are based on the theory that gold is 'grown,' and that the alchemist can, through his art, complete the process infinitely more quickly than Nature can, left to herself; but one suggests a transformation of 'primitive' gold to gold, while the other indicates the creation of an accelerator of transformation.)

Aristotle suggested that metals were produced within the earth by the action of vapour. Alchemists elaborated this idea, inferring that the warmth of the sun and the influence of the planets activate this vapour, and that because these factors vary according to the climate, the seasons, and the planetary configurations, so the types of metals laid down in the earth will vary. In the alchemical process they sought to imitate this, by taking the degree of heat in the furnace, the time of year, and the astro-logical indications into account. By observing Nature, the wise handmaid of the divine Will, the alchemist could begin to understand her ways, it was said, and learn how to imitate and improve on them through Art.

The alchemist's view of the earth was of a living organism that was in a constant state of change and growth. In alchemy there is no such thing as 'dead' matter; all substance has life and movement. This view is echoed by a modern geologist:

> Over the whole earth, throughout its rocky crust, physical, chemical and electrical forces are together engaged in producing movement of matter, in breaking down combinations already formed, and in building up new mineral combinations from the ruins of those previously existing.

> Below the oxidized zone the rocks may be considered as alive, for the activities working within such rock-masses are only comparable to functions of living organisms.

> Water in all cases appears to be the transporting agent, whether carrying a molecule of matter in chemical combination through a compact rock; as a waterspout trundling immense rocks, tons in weight, down a steep slope; or as ice moving matter on land or afloat. It appears to be the universal motive force, acting chemically or mechanically. It is all-pervading, for even igneous rocks contain an appreciable quantity of water in their composition.[7]

Early Western alchemy, then, in the first centuries AD, contained most of the key themes developed by later alchemists. Its theory of transformation was based on the classical concept of the elements, and on the philosophy of an ever-active power of Nature that was present as a living spirit in every atom of matter. Its processes were described in cryptic and symbolic terms, which may have been a convention originating with the secrecy of metal craft, but which clearly indicated that the work had a psychic as well as a physical dimension. As we shall see in the following chapter, alchemy was already thought to be based on revelation rather than on the accumulation of data, and acquiring the secrets of alchemy was equated with achieving understanding of the laws of universal harmony.

Eastern Alchemy: The Search for the Elixir

Although this book is concerned chiefly with tracing the Western tradition of alchemy, a brief look will now be taken at the early practice of alchemy in the East, so that the parallels and differences between the two may be noted. In many ways, the development of alchemy in the Far East is remarkably similar to that of alchemy in the West, especially in the first thousand years of their existence. Scholars are not able to agree about the reasons for this. Some argue that alchemy began in the East and was transmitted by connections as yet untraced to the West, while some consider the reverse to be more likely. Others, such as H. J. Shepperd,[7] argue for independent origins in East and West, with possible cross-fertilization at a later stage, such as a Chinese influence on Arabian alchemy in the seventh century AD. Shepperd points out that metallurgic skills developed independently in different cultures as a natural part of human evolution, and that these involved a secrecy and mystery that would have given rise to alchemical work almost spontaneously. There are differences of emphasis in the Eastern and Western histories of alchemy, even though both sought the transformation of earthly materials into a divine potency. In the West, the quest was primarily concerned with the transmutation of gold, whether for physical or spiritual purposes. In the East, alchemists aspired to make a perfect elixir of gold, which would bring immortality to the soul and supernatural powers to the mind, such as the ability to tap the knowledge of the celestial beings:

> My teacher also used to say that if one wished for perpetual life one should diligently take the great medicines, and that if one desired to communicate with the gods and spirits one should use solutions of metals and practice the multiplication of one's person. By multiplying the person one will be able automatically to see the three hun souls and the seven pho souls within one's body. One will also be able to enter the presence of the powers and principalities of the

heavens, and the deities of the earth, as well as having the spirits of all the mountains and rivers in one's service.[8]

Alchemy in the East, as in the West, also had a materialistic and naive aspect. Many alchemists hoped that the elixir would grant them physical immortality—or, at the very least, life for many centuries. This inspired certain kings in the fourth century BC to send envoys in search of the magical mountain isles where the immortal beings were thought to reside, presumably to wrest their secrets from them.

Gold was venerated in the East from ancient times. One of the Indian Vedas, written around the eighth century BC, mentions the use of a golden talisman to prolong life, and from the seventh century BC comes the saying: 'Gold is indeed fire, light, and immortality.' The first real records of alchemy date from the first few centuries AD, parallelling Western development. It is known that alchemy was practised in India, Tibet, and Burma, but the best information available to us concerns China (due mainly to the researches of Joseph Needham).

Alchemy in China had its roots in Taoism, a branch of religious philosophy whose greatest sage is considered to be Lao Tsu, author of the *Tao Te Ching* (probably sixth century BC). The 'way' of Taoism affirms that life is a ceaseless flow of changes and transmutations. The Tao is the spirit that gives rise to all, and contains within itself both light and dark, male and female, *yin* and *yang*.

> The Tao begot one. One begot two.
> Two begot three.
> And three begot ten thousand things.
> The ten thousand things carry yin and embrace yang.
> They achieve harmony by combining these forces.[9]

Students of the Tao were encouraged to live with Nature and find knowledge through simple tasks and manual work, in direct contrast to the rival, speculative school of Confucianism. It is thought that alchemy, along with yogic and sexual disciplines, were practised by Taoist students as a way of learning to bring natural energies into harmony. Taoism was very free in its approach, maintaining that our knowledge of truth is always relative and conditioned by the times we live in, and that new ideas and formulations are often helpful. The emphasis upon experiment, observation of Nature, and practical disciplines accorded well with the spirit of alchemy.

Other Taoist concepts that resonated with alchemical ideas concerned the power of water and the mystery of the Tao itself. The *Tao Te Ching* says:

> The highest good is like water.
> Water gives life to the ten thousand things and does not strive.
> It flows in places men reject and so is like the Tao.

Water is often described as the universal medium in alchemy; the primal material of alchemy is defined in similar terms to the power of the Tao. In both alchemy and Taoism, there seems to be an idea of a Spirit in all things that is greater than anything else in the world, and yet ignored by all:

> The great Tao flows everywhere, both to the left and to the right.
> The ten thousand things depend upon it; it holds nothing back.
> It fulfills its purpose silently and makes no claim.
>
> It nourishes the ten thousand things,
> And yet is not their lord.
> It has no aim; it is very small.
>
> The ten thousand things return to it,
> Yet it is not their lord.
> It is very great.
>
> It does not show greatness,
> And is therefore truly great.[‡]

Alchemy in China absorbed other elements of the prevailing culture and philosophies. The school of the Naturalists (*c.* 350–270 BC) promoted an interest in science and the discovery of the properties of matter. Five elements were said to compose the basis of the material world: they were called earth, wood, metal, fire, and water. These did not have quite the same connotations as the classical Western elements, and appear to have

---

‡ compare this with the description of the first material on p. 62.

defined qualities of plasticity and permeability. The element of wood, for instance, was said to represent that quality in matter which determines whether a surface is curved or straight; the element of metal was taken as the property of a substance that allows melting and moulding to take place.

Alchemy in the West used astrology as a guide to the correct timing of events; Chinese alchemy did the same, and added the use of the *I Ching*, the Book of Changes. This is a divinatory text, still much used and admired today, that describes how the changes in the seasons, in societies, and in man himself come about.

Chinese alchemy did not restrict itself solely to the preparation of the Elixir, but also embodied a quest for transmutation of metals as a subsidiary interest. Huan T'an, in the first century BC, was said to have had a drug that would convert quicksilver into gold. Neither were charlatans restricted to Western alchemy; we may infer their existence in China from an edict published around 144 BC commanding public execution of all those who were counterfeiting gold.

Laboratory experiment was an intrinsic part of Eastern alchemical practice. This led to the understanding of various chemical principles and by about the third century BC, the Taoists had already grasped the technique of condensation. In the fourth century AD an emperor set up a Taoist laboratory to conduct alchemical experiments. This particular establishment had a rather curious aspect to it, however; condemned criminals were used as guinea pigs to test the elixirs that the industrious alchemists produced! One wonders whether this was a cruel and cowardly procedure, or a generous gesture to give the condemned men one last chance!

DREAMS AND REVELATIONS

How did alchemists acquire their knowledge? There were teachers, manuscripts, and, later, printed books from which they might learn. But accounts of alchemical discoveries frequently relate that the key to the mystery was found through a personal vision or revelation. It was also emphasized that such illumination could only come to those who were sincere, persistent, and well-prepared to receive the secret knowledge:

> A most wonderful Magistery and Archmagistery is the Tincture of sacred Alchemy, the marvellous science of the secret Philosophy, the singular gift bestowed upon men through the grace of Almighty God—which men have never discovered through the labour of their own hands, but only by revelation and the teaching of Others.[1]

This idea of a direct, personal revelation, frequently expressed through a vision or dream, is worth careful consideration, for it clarifies many of the aspects of alchemy which at first seem bewildering. It sheds light on why alchemical descriptions are nearly always given in terms of verbal or pictorial symbols, and it helps us to understand why no one account of the alchemical process ever seems to follow exactly the same lines as another. Even allowing for the difference between individual schools of alchemy, the fact is that each alchemist demonstrates his art in an original way; just as no person's dream is ever exactly the same as another's.

The philosophy operating here is that *knowledge exists,* and that we can attune ourselves to receive it. Individual consciousness can link into a consciousness of a higher order and can learn from it. Knowledge revealed in this way is unlikely to surface in a precise or literal form, however; it exists at the level of what we call archetypes, a level of principle and abstract understanding. It will thus be received more as the seed of an idea, something that can be developed, worked on, and given an external application. Moreover, a person will receive and understand an idea according to his own cultural background and the age in which he lives. Knowledge is like a pool; a man dips his pitcher into the pool and the water he carries away adapts itself to the form of this particular container.

Alchemy is not unique in transmitting a tradition of personal revelation as a means of penetrating the mysteries of the world. Probably all religions embody accounts of dreams, visions, and encounters with divine messengers that bring wisdom and understanding—Moses on the mountain, the annunciation to the Virgin Mary, and the Book of Revelations are obvious examples from the Bible alone. It is generally accepted that the most profound religious understanding is likely to come through revelation and internal illumination. It is less commonly considered that knowledge can also arise in this way in relation to many other aspects of life. We have become used to the idea that 'facts' and 'theories' are built up only through a process of trial and error and planned experiment. Yet, it seems, this is far from the truth, even in science, as A. M. Taylor points out: 'The history of science shows us, again and again, great discoveries made by passionate adherence to ideas forged in the white heat of imagination.'[2]

Arts and sciences alike rely on inspiration, as we may loosely call it. Many artists, writers, and musicians feel as though they are giving concrete expression to what already exists; their talents lie both in being receptive to the 'inspiration' and in possessing the skills to interpret it in terms of colours, words, notes, and so on.

A. M. Taylor points out that some of the most important scientific ideas did *not* fit the facts as they could be demonstrated, and that the scientists concerned had to persist with their visions, despite the apparent evidence, until the data available could expand to demonstrate the truth of their theories.

In *The Case for Astrology*, J. A. West and J. G. Toonder argue that the zodiac arose from direct understanding, rather than being built up empirically:

Scholars suppose, though upon no evidence, that astrology 'evolved' piecemeal and fortuitously just as they suppose organic life to have done.

But whatever may be the value of the theory of evolution when applied to organic life, when applied to the development of ideas, religions or even superstitions it is a manifest impossibility . . .

In the realm of man, nothing evolves mindlessly.

No coherent body of knowledge—such as astrology—simply accumulates, taking form as it goes.

Works of art, religions, scientific hypotheses, train schedules—all must be *thought* of. And only then can they be brought into existence—the perfection or imperfection of the manifestation depending upon the expertise of the creator and the basic validity of the idea. But without that idea, nothing can happen.[3]

But while the science of today may be shy of admitting the power of the Idea, and even more wary of ascribing its birth to the activity of a higher form of consciousness, alchemy had no such scruples, and indeed the alchemists believed that their art could never be mechanical and could only be accomplished through access to a source of wisdom. (Even those who were taught by a living adept held, by and large, to the idea that 'the master will come when the pupil is ready'.) The chief medium of alchemical revelation, the way in which the 'Idea' surfaced into consciousness, seems to have been that of the vision. The *Corpus Hermeticum*, the body of hermetic writings originating from the early centuries of the Christian era and including alchemical, astrological, and metaphysical themes (see p. 99), begins thus:

> Once upon a time, when I had begun to think about the things that are, and my thoughts had soared high aloft, while my bodily senses had been put under restraint by sleep—yet not such sleep as that of men weighed down by fullness of food or by bodily weariness—methought there came to me a Being of vast and boundless magnitude, who called me by name, and said to me, 'What do you wish to hear and see, and to learn and to come to know by thought?' 'Who are you?' I said. 'I,' said he, 'am Poimandres, the Mind of the Sovereignty.' 'I would feign learn,' said I, 'the things that are, and understand their nature, and get knowledge of God.'

The dreamer is then taught about the role of the elements of nature in the creation of the world.

One of the most famous visionary alchemical accounts was written by Zosimos and included in his work *On Virtue* (fourth century AD). When we read alchemical writings expressed as dreams or visions, it is impossible to say, of course, whether they represent an exact account of the vision as it appeared to the alchemist, or whether the original revelation has been filled out and worked through to a more comprehensible stage, just as an artist will develop a painting from an original sketch. Doubtless this will vary from author to author. But it is obvious that there is a true tradition of alchemical knowledge surfacing through dreams and visions, and the quality of the images described is certainly like those experienced in profound dreams, rather than according with a 'literary' attempt to write a dream. The vision of Zosimos now follows:

Lesson One - *Of Virtue*

'The composition of the waters, the movement, increase, removal and restitution of the corporeal nature, the separation of the spirit from the body and the fixing of the spirit in the body—these are the operations which do not depend upon adding foreign substances but on the essential and unique nature of the material, which is self-activating and derives from one single species, such as hard, solidified minerals and liquid extracted from plants. This whole system, both single and many-coloured in its nature, comprises a multiple and infinitely varied research, a research into nature, which is subject to the influence of the moon and of the measure of time, the factors which rule the term of growth through which nature makes its transformation.'

Saying these things, I fell asleep, and I saw a sacrificing priest who stood above me by an altar shaped like a chalice. The altar had fifteen steps leading up to it. The priest stood up, and I heard a loud voice from above which said to me, 'I have completed the act of descending the fifteen steps, walking into darkness, and the act of climbing the steps towards the light. It is the sacrificer who renews me by rejecting the denseness of the body. Thus, consecrated a priest by necessity, I become a spirit.'

Having heard the voice of him who stood above on the chalice-shaped altar, I demanded to know who he was. And he, in a shrill voice replied thus: 'I am Ion, the priest of the sanctuaries, and I have undergone intolerable violence. Someone came suddenly in the morning and he took me by force, cleaving me in two with a sword, dismembering me, following the rules of combination. He took off all the skin from my head with the sword which he held, he mixed my bones with my flesh, and he burnt them in the fire of the process. It was thus that I learnt, through the transformation of the body, to become a spirit, so intolerable was the violence.' As I forced him to speak to me thus, his eyes became like blood and he vomited up all his flesh. And I saw him take the appearance of a tiny man, tearing himself with his own teeth and falling away.

Filled with fear, I woke up and I thought, 'Is this not the composition of the waters?' I told myself that I had understood this well, and I fell asleep again. I saw the same chalice-shaped altar and in its highest part water boiling and many people carried about endlessly by this water. And there was no one outside the altar whom I could ask about this. So I climbed up to the altar to see this spectacle. And I saw a little man, a barber whitened by age who said to me: 'What are you looking at?' I answered that I was surprised to see the activation of the water and the men burnt yet living. He replied to me in this way. 'This spectacle which you see is the entrance, the exit, and the change.' I asked him, 'What change?' and he replied, 'It is the place of the operation called mortification; for the men who wish to partake of the virtue enter in here and become spirits, having left the body.' Then I said, 'Are you a spirit?' And he answered, 'Yes, a spirit and a guardian of spirits.' During our conversation the boiling increased and the people shrieked lamentably, and I saw a man of copper holding a lead tablet in his hand. He spoke the following words unto me, while looking at the tablet: 'I counsel those who are being punished to calm themselves, to take each one a tablet of lead, to write on it in their own hand, to keep their eyes fixed upwards and their mouths open, until the grapes are ready to be gathered.' The act followed the word and the master of the house said to me: 'You have contemplated, you have stretched up your neck and you have seen what is done.' I replied that I had seen this, and he said, 'That which you see is the man of copper; he is the chief of the priests and of the sacrifice, he who vomits his own flesh. He has been given authority over this water and over the people to be punished.'

After seeing this apparition, I woke up again. I said, 'What is the meaning of this vision? Is this not the divine water, this white and yellow boiling water?' And I knew that I had understood. I said that it is good both to speak and to listen, to give and to receive, to be poor and to be rich. Otherwise, how can nature learn to give and to receive? The man of copper gives, and the liquified stone receives; the mineral gives and the plant receives; the thunder claps give out the fire which leaps out from them. In the chalice of the altar, all things blend and all separate; all unite, all combine, all mix and part; all things are moistened and dried, all things flower and shed their flowers. In essence, for each one it is through the method, measure, and exact weight of the four elements that the blending and separating of all things occur; no liaison happens without a process taking place. It is a natural process, breathing in and out, preserving forms and increasing and diminishing them. In a word, when all things are brought to agreement by division and union, without neglecting the process, nature is transformed; for nature, returning to herself, transforms herself, and this concerns the quality and the bond of virtue throughout the whole universe.

In brief, my friend, build a temple of one stone, resembling white lead, alabaster, with no beginning nor end in its construction. It should have within it a source of pure water, sparkling like the sun. Observe carefully on which side of the temple the entrance lies, and, taking a sword in your hand, seek out the entrance, for the opening is narrow indeed. A serpent sleeps at the entrance, guarding the temple. Seize him, and sacrifice him; skin him, and, taking his flesh and bones, dismember him. Then reunite his parts with his bones at the entrance to the temple, and, making a step of him, climb up and enter; you will find there that which you seek. The priest, this man of copper, whom you will see seated in the spring, mustering his colour, should not be thought of as a man of copper, for he has changed the colour of his nature and become a man of silver. If you wish, you will soon have him as a man of gold.

Zosimos himself gives guidance as to how the imagery of the dream may be interpreted in alchemical terms—representing separating, combining, moistening, and transforming. Anyone at all sensitive to imagery will see that the vision described has far more power than that of a mere chemical experiment put into colourful terms. For alchemists, what is true on a physical, or chemical, level is also true at the emotional and spiritual level. The work of the alchemist is to achieve transformation on all three levels at once. Thus it becomes clear why the language of dreams and visions is such an appropriate medium for alchemy, for the symbols can contain all three levels of meaning at once.

Another well-known alchemical vision is that of George Ripley, who lived in the fifteenth century. In *The Twelve Gates* he wrote:

When busie at my Book I was upon a certain Night,
This *Vision* here exprest appear'd unto my dimmed sight:
A Toad full Ruddy I saw, did drink the juice of Grapes so fast,
Till over-charged with the broth, his Bowels all to brast:
And after that, from poyson'd Bulk he cast his Venom fell,
For Grief and Pain whereof his Members all began to swell;
With drops of poysoned sweat aproaching thus his secret Den,
His Cave with blasts of fumous Air he all bewhited then:
And from the which in space a Golden Humour did ensue,
Whose falling drops from high did stain the soyl with ruddy hue.

And when his Corps the force of vital breath began to lack,
This dying Toad became forthwith like Coal for colour Black:
Thus drowned in his proper veins of poysoned flood;
For term of Eighty days and Four he rotting stood
By Tryal then this Venom to expel I did desire;
For which I did commit his Carkass to a gentle Fire:
Which done, a Wonder to the sight, but more to be rehearst;
The Toad with Colours rare through every side was pierc'd,
And White appear'd when all the sundry hews were past:
Which after being tincted Ruddy, for evermore did last.
Then of the Venom handled thus a Medicine I did make;
Which Venom kills, and saveth such as Venom chance to take:
Glory be to him the granter of such secret ways,
Dominion, and Honour both, with Worship, and with Praise.
AMEN.

The alchemical process is unfolded through this sequence. The first matter, the Toad (an image which is in accordance with the idea that the first matter may be despised and rejected by men because of its outer appearance), is fed with alchemical water until it bursts (separates) and releases its spirit while the body putrefies (the *nigredo*). Then it is reheated and the 'Peacock's Tail' stage of many colours occurs, being followed by whitening and then reddening, which is the formation of the Tincture, or Stone.

Perhaps it may seem to the reader too neat that a fully-fledged symbolic account of the alchemical process should arise in George Ripley's head as he pored over his books. Most dreams, after all, appear far less unified and coherent. But, in the context of alchemy, we should think of visions as states for which the practitioner actively strove. It is possible to induce and affect dreams deliberately. Although this faculty has been known in various societies and traditions from time immemorial, modern psychology has only recently rediscovered the ability, and people with psychological problems or interested in self-development are now being encouraged to take an active part in their own dreams. Certain recurrent features in dreams can, for instance, be investigated and confronted by the dreamer, and periods of 'lucid' dreaming (being aware that one is dreaming) can be extended to exercise control over the direction of the dream. An alchemist seeking a revelation, and focussing his mind through prayer, study, and the contemplation of alchemical imagery, is deliberately setting up conditions in which an illuminating dream can arise more readily.

Additionally, dreams may be encouraged to unfold while one is awake. Again, this technique has been known for centuries but is only now re-emerging into general awareness; it is often called 'guided imagery' or 'pathworking.' The imaginative faculty is allowed to work as internal vision, either moving freely or else focussing on a set theme, such as following a pathway, visiting a garden, entering a castle, and so on. A certain level of awareness must persist, or else images disintegrate into fragmented daydreams; this is why the exercise is often carried out in groups, or with a trained leader. Images that arise this way when the exercise is tackled correctly often have much of the stirring quality of dream imagery, or even of mythology, but usually lack the confusion of dreams or the inconsequentiality of daydreams.

It is probable that alchemists took the pursuit of vision to this active stage. Ripley, it may be noted, said that his sight was 'dimmed' but not that he was sleeping. Even more telling are the words of John Dastin, whose alchemical poem, *Dastin's Dream*, begins:

> Not yet full sleeping, nor yet full waking, But between the twain
> lying in a trance;
> Halfe closed mine Eyes in my slumbering . . .
> Towards Aurora, ere Phoebus uprise,
> I dreamed one came to me to do me pleasaunce
> That brought me a book with seven seals close . . .

> Following upon I had a wonderful dream,
> As seemed to my inward thought,
> The face of him shone as the sun beam:
> Which unto me this heavenly book brought,
> Of so great riches that it may not be bought.

The visions of the alchemists, it would seem, hovered between the levels of sleep, semiconsciousness, and the waking state, sometimes triggered by long hours spent poring over books or prolonged periods of concentration as they watched the alchemical vessels for signs of change. Some may have come unbidden, as welcome but unexpected revelations which brought the insight that was needed; others may have been induced deliberately. Cornelius Agrippa, magician, philosopher, and alchemist of the sixteenth century, described how men may prepare themselves to receive significant dreams:

> Now I call that a dream, which proceedeth either from the spirit of the phantasie and intellect united together, or by the illustration of the Agent intellect above our souls, or by the true revelation of some divine power in a quiet and purified mind; for by this our soul receiveth true oracles, and abundantly yieldeth prophecies to us: for in dreams we seem both to Ask questions, and learn to read and find them out . . . It is necessary, that he who should receive true dreams, should keep a pure, undisturbed, and an undisquieted imaginative spirit, and so compose it, that it may be made worthy of the knowledge and government by the mind and understanding . . . when therefore we are found in body, not disturbed in mind, not dulled by meat or drink, nor sad through poverty, nor provoked by any vice or lust or wrath, but chastly going to bed, fall asleep, then our pure and divine soul being loosed from all hurtfull thoughts, and now freed by dreaming, is endowed with this divine spirit as an instrument, and doth receive those beams and representations, which are darted down, and shine forth from the divine minde into it self; and as it were in a deifying glass, it doth far more certainly, clearly, and efficaciously behold all things, then by the Vulgar enquiry of the intellect, and by the discourse of reason . . .[4]

To whom or to what did the alchemists ascribe their visions? They knew that what they saw and experienced came from a greater source of power than that of their own imaginations. Many gladly gave thanks to God for the illumination they had received. But many also perceived a guide or spirit who acted as a medium for the vision. The author of the Hermetic text obtained his knowledge from Poimandres, 'the Mind of the Sovereignty,' seen as a great being. Another work, dating from the Arabic period of alchemy, but possibly having earlier origins, is entitled *The Book of Thirty Chapters*, and here the vision is granted by an unnamed being, possibly Hermes Trismegistus (the 'patron saint' of alchemy):

> When I realized that love of the Great Work had fallen into my heart and that the preoccupations I felt about it had chased sleep from my eyes, that they prevented me from eating and drinking so that my body was wasting away and my appearance was bad, I gave myself up to prayer and fasting. I begged God to drive out the miseries and

> cares that had taken hold of my heart, and put an end to the per-
> plexed situation in which I found myself.
>
> While I lay asleep on my couch, a being appeared to me in a dream
> and told me, 'Rise up and understand what I am going to show
> you.'
>
> I rose up and went off with this person. Soon we arrived before
> Seven Gates so fine that I had never seen the like. 'Here,' my guide
> said to me, 'are found the treasures of the science you seek.'
>
> 'Thank you,' I replied. 'Now guide me so that I may penetrate into
> these dwellings where you say are found the treasures of the uni-
> verse.'
>
> 'You will never penetrate there,' he answered, 'unless you have in
> your power the keys of those doors. But come with me. I'll show you
> the keys of those doors.'

Each door corresponds to a metal associated with a planet and the aspirant is given teaching at each one. (The notion of seven gates to be passed
through is strongly reminiscent of the Mithraic tradition, where initiates
had to pass through seven realms ruled by planets in order to return to the
source of all creation.) He is taught the relationship between body, soul,
and spirit, and between the elements, and is instructed in many other
aspects of alchemy through word and emblem. Finally, another guide, an
old man, shows him a three-bodied animal, the 'Key of Science,' whose
parts devour one another.

> The old man said to me, 'Man, go and find that animal, give him an
> intelligence in place of yours, a vital spirit in place of yours, a life in
> place of yours; then he'll submit to you and give you all you need.'
>
> As I wondered how I could give anyone an intelligence in place of
> mine, a vital spirit in place of mine, an existence in place of mine, the
> old man said, 'Take the body that is like your own, take from it what
> I have just told you, and hand it over to him.'
>
> I did as the old man bade me, and I acquired then the whole sci-
> ence, as complete as that described by Hermes.[5]

Zosimos formulated a philosophy of revelation, suggesting that there was
a universal being of man, with body, soul, and spirit, and that it is this
'Great Man' who comes in various guises to teach the individual:

In effect the Nous, our god, declares: 'The Son of God, who can do all things and become all things as he wishes, shows himself as he wishes to each man.

And up to this day, and on till the end of the world, in secret and in hidden ways, he comes to those who are his and communicates with them, counselling them, in secret and by means of their intellect, to separate themselves from their Adam,§ who blinds them and who grudges the spiritual and luminous man.'

Nicholas Flamel, the fourteenth-century alchemist whom we shall meet again later, saw his guiding light as an angel, who appeared to him while he was in a deep sleep, showing him an ancient and handsome volume, and telling him that he would one day understand its contents. Later he found this very book on sale and discovered it to be an old alchemical manuscript.

One of the most curious alchemical stories in which the aspirant seeks guidance comes from the pen of Bolos, a Greek alchemist who lived around AD 200. He tells us that his teacher was Ostanes, who died before he could finish his instruction. Bolos decided to summon up the spirit of his worthy master; succeeding in this, he demands alchemical information from Ostanes. Ostanes remains silent during this badgering, and only when addressed more respectfully does he choose to speak, telling Bolos, 'The books are in the temple.' Bolos and his fellow students search the temple thoroughly but find nothing. Some time later, they are enjoying a banquet in the temple when suddenly one of the columns splits open. They rush to see if the sacred tomes are hidden inside, but they find no books, only one simple formula: 'A nature is delighted by another nature, a nature conquers another nature, a nature dominates another nature.' This, said Bolos, gave them the key to the alchemical art; the saying was also held in great reverence by later alchemists.

It is clear from the alchemical accounts that the Great Work was seen as having a divine origin, and that it was thought necessary to obtain teaching through a great sage, living or dead, or through a direct vision that would serve as a basis for the work. It is little wonder, then, that we find gods, goddesses, and Biblical and mythical sages claimed as founders of the art. Perhaps the boldest claim is that God gave 'the medicine' to Adam, and that it was passed from him to the chosen few who have perpetuated a line of succession. In the early days of alchemy, in particular, it was implied that

§ Adam is the base and ignorant aspect of man.

the perfect knowledge of alchemy could be found hidden in one very special book, or inscribed on a column in a certain temple. Sometimes the all-important text was thought to be hidden in the tomb of a king. Alchemists from the fifteenth to the seventeenth century in Europe dwelt on the same theme, but usually expressed it in terms of the constant search by the student for the one *right* book among the hundreds of fraudulent and mendacious texts available. It is the myth of the perfect knowledge, once known, and now nearly lost, lingering still in an obscure, secret, or hidden place.

The alchemists, however, did not sit back and wait hopefully for revelatory insights. They knew that they had to work, study, and experiment in their laboratories and follow a thousand false trails before they could prove themselves worthy of discovering the true alchemical practice. They had to take the risk that they might never find it, and that they might end their days in poverty and social ostracism.

> Our Art, its theory as well as its practice, is altogether a gift of God, Who gives it when and to whom He elects . . . Though I had diligently studied this Art for seventeen or eighteen years, yet I had, after all, to wait for God's own time, and accept it as a free gift. No one need doubt the truth or certainty of this Art. It is as true and certain, and as surely ordained by God in nature, as it is that the sun shines at noon-tide, and the moon shews forth her soft splendour at night.[6]

In the later centuries of alchemy, especially in the sixteenth and seventeenth centuries, there seem to be fewer accounts of direct visions, perhaps partly because alchemical authors of this period were keen to introduce more philosophical discourse into their works. But the visionary *quality* lived on, and was often deliberately introduced in the form of parables or allegories, as in the lengthy *The Chymical Wedding of Christian Rosenkreutz* (see p. 63). Michael Maier wrote *A Subtle Allegory concerning the Secrets of Alchemy,* described—truly for once—as 'very useful to possess and pleasant to read.' It tells the story of a traveler in search of the miraculous Phoenix that would change grief and anger to gold. And some of the famous sequences of visual images and commentaries, such as *The Book of Lambspring,* retain the fresh and spontaneous quality of dream symbolism.

It may be that alchemical accounts of visions have had a wider influence in the field of literature, and that other writers found in this visionary form a framework for their allegories. Langland's *Piers Plowman,* written in the fourteenth century, begins with the narration of Piers as he falls asleep by the side of the stream: 'And I dreamt a marvellous dream: I was in a wilderness, I could not tell where, and looking Eastwards I saw a tower high up against the sun, and splendidly built on top of a hill; and far beneath it was a great gulf, with a dungeon in it, surrounded by deep, dark pits, dreadful to see . . .' Even closer to the alchemical genre is John Bunyan's *Pilgrim's Progress* (1675), which traces the journey of the pilgrim who wishes to reach salvation and charts the crises and stages of transformation he must go through before reaching the Holy City. It starts: 'As I walked through the wilderness of this world, I lighted on a certain place where there was a den, and laid me down in that place to sleep; and as I slept, I dreamed a dream. . .' It has a great deal in common with the alchemical process, since it begins with Christian's struggle with the Slough of Despond, the 'scum and filth' of the world, that equates with the base First Matter of the alchemists. It ends, as does the Great Work, with gold, in the Celestial City:

> So I saw that when they awoke [Christian and Hope] they addressed themselves to go up to the city. But, as I said, the reflection of the sun upon the city (for the city was pure gold. . .) was so extremely glorious, that they could not, as yet, with open faces behold it, but through an instrument made for that purpose. So I saw that, as they went on, there met them two men in raiment that shone like gold, also their faces shone as the light . . .

EMBLEMS OF KNOWLEDGE

The story of alchemy now passes from its inception among the Greeks and Egyptians to its full flowering in Western Europe from the thirteenth to the seventeenth centuries. This chapter, and the three that follow, will explore certain aspects of alchemy during the four centuries of its heyday; the order of the chapters bears some relation to the historical chronology. This chapter deals with the symbols, terms, and images used in alchemy, a pattern of communication that was established in the medieval period. The succeeding chapter examines the alchemist himself, his training, his laboratory, and his public image, and this will span the whole period in question. The following two chapters dwell primarily on the later period, the sixteenth and seventeenth centuries: the first looks at the tradition of spiritual alchemy, which was then at its most evolved stage, the second at alchemy's influence upon literature, science, and medicine.

From Islam to Medieval Europe

Alchemy was transmitted to Europe by the Arabs, who, from the seventh century onwards, devoted much time and study not only to alchemy but also to mathematics, astronomy, and astrology. The rise of the new religion, Islam, founded by the prophet Mohammed, gave a strong focus for the Arab tribes and enabled them to consolidate their identity; from this new unity arose conditions favourable to learning and experiment. The Arabs expanded their Islamic Empire into Spain in the eighth century, and this, though it was the cause of strife, enabled Arabic teachings and ideas to pass more easily into the rest of Europe. The Arabs translated many ancient alchemical works from the Greek, and certain Greek texts have come down to us today only through their Arabic versions, making it difficult for scholars to verify and date the original material. The most famous Arabian alchemists known to us are Khalid ibn Yazid (d. 704), Abu Musa Jabir (fl 760), and Al-Razi (b. *c* 864). **Khalid** was a prince who lived at Damascus, and it is reported that he was the first Moslem to take an interest in alchemy. A famous story concerning him (which cannot, unfortunately, be proved) is that he summoned to his palace every person who professed some alchemical knowledge, but found that neither he nor they could achieve anything resembling a transmutation of metals. He was then visited by a Christian hermit from Jerusalem, named Morienus, who arrived with the intention of converting Khalid to Christianity. However, when he found that Khalid's only desire was to transmute gold, he carried out the alchemical miracle before the prince's eyes. Khalid immediately ordered the execution of all the other alchemists who had failed him, and Morienus (wisely, perhaps) fled from the palace and could not be found. Khalid sent his envoys out to search for him, and eventually, after many years, Morienus was found and persuaded to return. The legend ends with the satisfying finale that Khalid was then initiated into the mysteries of alchemy, and went on to write books and poems about the art. Whether or not the whole story is true, we do know that certain alchemical writings ascribed to Khalid were listed by later alchemists, and some are still extant today, even though the authorship is not beyond dispute.

The controversy surrounding writings ascribed to Jabir, often called **Geber**, is even greater. He was venerated by the later European alchemists more than any other Arabic writer, and it is probable that a Geber school or tradition carried on his work and used his name to head some of the later texts they produced. Abu Musa Jabir lived in the eighth century; he was a member of a South Arabian tribe and came to Arabia from Persia due to political unrest. It is said that he studied with certain important religious leaders of the day and that he became a Sufi, a member of that mystical and esoteric sect that flourished within Islam. As well as alchemy, he studied and explored medicine, warfare, and music, and we know that he found favour at court for much of his life as a respected scholar. His most influential ideas were probably those that updated the Aristotelian theory of the elements. Aristotle maintained that minerals are produced in the earth through an exhalation like 'earthy smoke,' and metals through one like 'watery vapour,' the former consisting of particles of earth changing into fire, the latter of water changing into air. Geber said that these exhalations passed through an intermediate stage of conversion. The earthy smoke changed into sulphur, the water vapour became mercury; the sulphur and mercury then combined in varying proportions to give minerals or metals. The perfect combination would produce gold. Geber knew very well that ordinary sulphur and mercury would not produce these effects, and he proposed that the sulphur and mercury with this power of formation are higher, rarefied versions of the common substances that we know.

Geber also introduced some of the Arabian love of numbers into alchemy. He worked out various complicated systems for calculating the right amounts of materials and substances to use in alchemical procedures that were based on the inherent and symbolic power of number rather than on practical considerations. He attempted to find the perfect balance of substances and elements and came nearer to the modern principles of chemical equations in his work than any other alchemist of this or later times. About a hundred books are ascribed to him, but it is certain that many of these are pseudographical. Some of the alchemical methods he describes are so complex and tortuous that his name unfortunately gave rise to the term 'gibberish'. There is a legend that about two hundred years after his death, his laboratory at Kufa was discovered as some houses were being demolished, exposing his work room and a golden mortar more than two pounds in weight!

AJ-Rhazi, also known as **Rhases**, was born around AD 864 and spent his life chiefly at Ray, near Teheran, with periods of work carried out at Baghdad. He is remembered as a man of great learning, specializing in medicine and alchemy, but also noted for his understanding of philosophy and for his skill as a musician. His writings on medicine stood the test of time until the sixteenth or seventeenth century, and in his day he was surrounded by many young students and visiting scholars whom he instructed. E. J. Holmyard quotes the following description of his teaching life:

> One of his biographers has drawn a graphic picture of Razi as an old man, seated on the paving of the courtyard of the hospital surrounded by his pupils. The advanced students sat in a ring nearest him, and in outer concentric rings sat those whom we might call the second-year and first-year men. Razi, the fount of wisdom at the centre, expounded to his immediate entourage, and the information, suitably simplified, was passed on to the less experienced.[1]

His works were great favourites with the European alchemists, even though he was interested primarily in practical chemistry, especially in the classification of substances and in improving laboratory technique. Although he followed Geber's theories with regard to mercury and sulphur and endeavoured to make elixirs with transmutatory properties, yet he did not rely solely on existing theories, preferring to experiment and try out new approaches. His laboratories were stocked with a sophisticated array of metals, minerals, and equipment.

Not many genuine Arab alchemical texts have been translated into English. The Islamic contribution to alchemy was very great and spanned several centuries, but specialist knowledge is needed to draw out its implications and to describe the complete tradition of alchemy that developed there. For the purposes of a book focusing on European alchemy, it is sufficient to note the importance of the Arabian influence, especially as a link between the Alexandrian and the European alchemical schools.

The Emerald Tablet

Early European alchemists seized eagerly upon any translations they could acquire of Arabian and Greek alchemical texts and based much of their work upon the principles laid down there. But for them, by far and away the most significant early text was the *Emerald Tablet of Hermes Trismegistus,* also called the *Tabula Smaragdina.* This was the alchemists' creed, the affirmation of their work, and a constant source of guidance and wisdom to them. It was sometimes engraved on the walls of the alchemical laboratory, and there can scarcely have been an alchemist who did not have the words written out or committed to memory.

There are several versions of the text, since it is known both in Latin and Arabic, and probably existed in Syriac and Greek forms before that. The translation commonly favoured by present-day scholars is that of R. Steele and D. W. Singer, made earlier this century, which runs as follows:

> True it is, without falsehood, certain and most true. That which is above is like to that which is below, and that which is below is like to that which is above, to accomplish the miracles of one thing.
>
> And as all things were by the contemplation of one, so all things arose from this one thing by a single act of adaptation.
>
> The father thereof is the Sun, the mother the Moon.
>
> The Wind carried it in its womb, the Earth is the nurse thereof.
>
> It is the father of all works of wonder throughout the whole world.
>
> The power thereof is perfect.
>
> If it be cast on to Earth, it will separate the element of Earth from that of Fire, the subtle from the gross.
>
> With great sagacity it doth ascend gently from Earth to Heaven.
>
> Again it doth descend to Earth, and uniteth in itself the force from things superior and things inferior.
>
> Thus thou wilt possess the glory of the brightness of the whole world, and all obscurity will fly from thee.

This thing is the strong fortitude of all strength, for it overcometh every subtle thing and doth penetrate every solid substance.

Thus was this world created.

Hence will there be marvellous adaptations achieved, of which the manner is this.

For this reason I am called Hermes Trismegistus, because I hold three parts of the wisdom of the whole world.

That which I had to say about the operation of Sol is completed.

No translations from the Latin text that I have seen differ radically from this rendering, and even an alternative Arabic text is similar in quality.[2] The Latin original is as follows:

Verum, sine mendacio, certum et verissimum.

Quod est inferius, est sicut [id] quod est superius, et quod est superius, est sicut [id]. quod est inferius, ad perpetranda miracula rei unius.

Et sicut omnes res fuerunt ab uno, meditatione, unius: sic omnes res natae feurunt ab hac una re, adaptione.

Pater ejus est Sol, mater ejus Luna: portavit illud ventus in ventre suo: nutrix ejus terra est.

Pater omnis thelesmi totius mundi est hic.

Vis [virtus] ejus integra est, si versa fuerit in terram.

Separabis terram ab igne, subtile a spisso, suaviter, cum magno ingenio.

Ascendit a terra in coelum, iterumquie descendit in terram, et recepit vim superiorum et inferiorum. Sic habebis gloriam totius mundi. Ideo fugiat [fugiet] a te omnis obscuritas.

Hic [haec] est totius fortudinis fortitudo fortis: quia vincet omnem rem subtilem, omnemque solidam penetrabit.

Sic mundus creatus est.

Hinc adaptiones erunt mirabiles, quarum modus est hic.

Itaque vocatus sum Hermes Trismegistus, habens tres partes Philosophiae totius mundi.

Completum est quod dixi de operatione Solis.[3]

It is likely that this text originates from the early centuries of the Christian era, in common with other writings ascribed to Hermes (see p. 99). But the European alchemists believed that the words came from the very dawn of time and were the original revelation of alchemy to man through the divine person of Hermes Trismegistus. 'Hermes saw the totality of things. Having seen he understood. Having understood, he had the power to reveal and show. And indeed what he knew, he wrote down. What he wrote, he mostly hid away, keeping silence rather than speaking out, so that every generation coming into the world had to seek out these things.'[4]

The name Hermes Trismegistus means Hermes the Thrice Great. In the general evolution of the classical deities, Hermes later became known as Mercury; but though Hermes and Mercury play somewhat similar roles in alchemy, they are not identical. Hermes was seen as the source of alchemical knowledge and was often thought to have been a real, though semi-divine, Egyptian adept. Mercury was the representation of the living spirit of alchemy, the volatile transforming power that could exalt matter into its most refined state.

Let us look, though, at the *Emerald Tablet* itself. Its appearance is surrounded by legend. Some said that it was found in the tomb of Hermes by Alexander the Great, while others declared that Sara, the wife of Abraham, discovered it in a secret cave. The usual theme is that it lay hidden in a cave, tomb, or chamber until a seeker worthy enough found it and brought it out so that the world might benefit from its wisdom. Many alchemists have written commentaries on it, implying that its meaning is highly enigmatic and needs deep study. It is possible for us to draw out certain key themes from it, however, and a simple interpretation in alchemical terms follows.

There is one Creator of all that exists. From his contemplation, all created forms have their source, arising through a process of adaptation or modification. The earthly world is created on the same principles as the heavenly, or spiritual, world. The primal energy is engendered by the male and female principles (sun and moon, and possibly fire and water) and brought to birth through air and earth. This energy, or 'first substance,' has the power to separate the subtle forces from the gross. It has the power to ascend and descend between the highest and the lowest, and to unite the two. It is the epitome of power and strength because it can penetrate both the subtlest and the grossest of substances.

The Alchemical Operation

Both would-be students of alchemy and researchers of the hermetic tradition have suffered tremendous frustration through trying to discern the sequence and method of the alchemical process. Alchemical texts and illustrations are fascinating, but they are also tantalizing, cryptic, and sometimes deliberately misleading in their descriptions. How true is the alchemical aphorism: 'Many search; few find'! There is a tragic ring to the story of poor old Tonsile, who had worked for sixty years without success, only to be rebuffed by the only alchemist he met who could have taught him the secret:

> Tonsile said I, what hould it you avail
> Such a thing to know? your limbs doth you fail
> For very age, therefore cease your lay;
> And love your beads, it is high time to pray;
> For if you knew the materials of our stone
> Ere you could make it your days would be gone.[5]

The basic theme of alchemy is that the first material is selected, prepared, and transformed through the correct process into the perfect Stone, which can then be used to perform miraculous functions, such as turning base metals into gold, or curing disease, prolonging life, or endowing the possessor with supernatural abilities. (It should be remembered, however, that the creator of the Stone and the Stone itself were one, to a great extent, and that the Stone could not necessarily be used in the same way by an outsider.) The first (primal) substance, which appears to be integrated and whole, must be separated into its components and reunited in a more harmonious manner. It must be purged of its baser elements in order that its higher form can appear. True transformation can come about only through death and rebirth, which means causing the first 'body' to die, and the 'soul' of the matter to ascend. Then the two can unite in a new manner, and grow to maturity, the volatile elements being fixed and made permanent and stable so that their properties can be used effectively. When these principles are grasped, alchemical emblems of battles, death, marriage, and generation can be better understood.

The order and number of the stages of the operation differ widely. It will be helpful to compare some examples, bearing in mind that each author puts his own seal of individuality on his work. *The Sum of Perfection (Summa)* by the pseudo-Geber (perhaps an early medieval author) gives a clear account of the laboratory operations and lists them in the following order:

1. *Sublimation*—'The elevation of a dry thing by fire, with adherence to its vessel.' This will remove the more obvious impurities from the first matter.

2. *Descension*—This is a further heating and purifying of the substance, which rests on a perforated support.

3. *Distillation*—The matter is heated; vapours are given off and allowed to condense and run back down again into the vessel, or into a separate receiver.

4. *Calcination*—'The pulverization of a thing by fire.' A further stage of purification, said to loosen the restricting 'sulphur' and free the 'mercury.'

5. *Solution*—'The reduction of a dry thing into water.' Special, acid liquids are used for this.

6. *Coagulation*—'The reduction of a thing liquid into a solid substance by privation of its humidity.' Again, fire would be used to drive off excess fluid.

7. *Fixation*—A process causing 'a fugitive thing to abide and sustain fire.'

8. *Ceration*—'The mollification of an hard thing, not fusible unto liquifaction.' This is a rendering of the matter to a waxlike consistency so that it is easier to use.

This rather mundane account has the advantage at least of helping us to understand the physical stages of the alchemical process.

In his *Twelve Gates,* George Ripley (fifteenth century) described the operation of alchemy in terms of a round castle with twelve entrances, each entrance signifying a stage to be completed. (The circular motif connects with the symbol of the Ouroboros—see p. 56—conveying the idea that the beginning and the end of the work are mysteriously linked, and that the operation is one and whole in its nature.) Ripley's version of the sequence has more symbolic overtones:

1. *Calcination*—This is a purgation of the first material, but it should not diminish its moisture, and therefore simple burning or corrosion is not what is required.

2. *Solution*—The matter is dissolved in a water that does not wet the hand. Everything should be carried out in one vessel only. Solution brings to light what is hidden.

3. *Separation*—The subtle is separated from the gross; earth remains below while the spirit flies up.

4. *Conjunction*—Natures contrary to one another (male and female, sulphur and mercury) are joined together. The vessel must be sealed, leaving the seed to develop until the time is right to feed the child that is born, the white stone.

5. *Putrefaction*—The bodies must be killed by heat so that regeneration can occur.

6. *Congelation*—A temperate heat is used to bring in the desired whiteness and to fix the spirits into the white stone.

7. *Cibation*—The dry matter must be fed with 'meat' and 'milk.' But do not overfeed it! Beware of 'dropsy' and 'the flood.'

8. *Sublimation*—A process lasting forty days to make the body spiritual and the spirit corporeal.

9. *Fermentation*—'Gold' with 'gold' must be fermented. This is to make it more active.

10. *Exaltation*—This is a similar process to sublimation, and Ripley indicates the power that is generated by quoting the Scriptures: 'Christ said, "If I exalted be, then shall I draw all things unto me."'

11. *Multiplication*—The elixir produced is increased in quantity, a process which does not involve manufacture of any extra elixir. (It is interesting to note that homeopathic medicines can be augmented by mixing the potentized remedy with water, which increases the volume without reducing the remedy's strength and efficacy.)

12. *Projection*—This is the use of the Stone for transformation.

It should be remembered that alchemy as a complete art involved physical processes at every stage, and although each stage had profound psychological and spiritual correspondences, which entered into the full completion of the work, yet each operation was carried out in the alchemist's laboratory with the use of the furnace, or athanor, with glass and pottery vessels, retorts, and all the other equipment that was available to the practising alchemist and chemist of the period. But the true alchemist, as opposed to the chemist, considered the symbolic aspect of his equipment to be of fundamental importance: he did not simply search for technical perfection through a proliferation of laboratory hardware. It is often stated, for instance, that the vessel in which the process is carried out should be round or egg-shaped. This symbolizes that it is 'one' in its nature, like the Creation, that it will help the Stone to attain the 'oneness' of its perfection, and the alchemist to find a 'oneness' of being. The vessel is round like a world in miniature, a cosmos in which creation takes place:

> For they [the adepts] being lovers of Wisdome more than worldly wealth drove at higher and more excellent operations: and certainly he to whom the whole court of nature lies open rejoiceth not so much that he can make gold and silver . . . as that he sees the heavens open, the angels of God ascending and descending, and that his own name is fairly written in the Book of Life.[6]

Examples from an alchemical sequence in which chemical and symbolical themes are combined are shown in the illustrations (pp. 51–54). These four stages come from the *Pleasure Garden of Chemistry*, written by Daniel Stolcius in 1624. Stolcius, a pupil of Michael Maier, came to England from his native Bohemia, which had been the centre of intense esoteric activity but which had then entered a period of political turbulence, forcing Stolcius to live in exile. The *Pleasure Garden of Chemistry* consists of 107 illustrations, each engraving accompanied by a poem written in Latin. The process itself is set out as a sequence of eleven stages: Calcination, Solution, Separation, Conjunction, Putrefaction, Congelation, Cibation, Sublimation, Fermentation, Exaltation, and Multiplication. Projection (the use of the Stone for transformation) may perhaps be a twelfth, unwritten, concluding stage. The first, second, fourth, and fifth steps are illustrated, and from the accompanying poems set out below, the reader will see how closely the pictures echo the written theme, even if the whole meaning is sometimes obscure!

Calcination Is the First Step of the Wise Ones

Mercurius sits happily
Winged at the table.
    He is guarded on both sides
    By sun and moon.

Upon this table, not by accident,
Grow herbs with flowers.
    The courageous lion unhesitatingly
    Devours the serpent.

Through powder the volatile spirit
Is generally fixed and made permanent.
    Then when put on its own soil
    It enjoys itself with fruit and flowers.

The Other Step Is the Disintegration of Solution

The hot lion promptly devours
The sun in the heavens.
    The beautiful nymph brings for this occasion
    Her tender flowers.

Then the fiery man will sweat
And become hot in the fire;
    Also he will resolve his body
    And carry it afar through moisture.

Expel the mastery accomplished
Through the mentioned powder's force,
    So that happily and beautifully
    Mercurius may issue therefrom.

The Fourth Step Is the Composition or Conjunction

After rain often appears
Beautiful, lovely sunshine;
    After anger comes again
    Much greater love.

What you have separated,
Unite again completely,
    So that many fertile seeds
    Bless you with many children.

In the meantime
Neptunus prepares a warm bath,
    So that husband and wife
    Wash their bodies clean.

The Fifth Step Is the Putrefaction

Destruction brings about
Death of the material;
    But the spirit renews,
    Like before, the life.

Hence the black globe
Signifies the black raven.
    Also the light spirit
    Quickly expels human consciousness;

Provided that the seed is
Putrefied in the right soil;
    Otherwise all labour, work, and art
    Will be in vain.[7]

The Primal Material

The alchemist must take some substance to start his operations. But what should his 'first matter' be? This is one of the most jealously guarded secrets of alchemy, and many an alchemical writer, while claiming to be utterly frank in all other respects, is evasive when it comes to naming the kind of material from which the Stone can be made. Since a fundamental alchemical idea is that the perfect Stone is created from something that is apparently base and worthless, it follows that the matter required is of necessity something that is overlooked and despised by men—'the corner stone which the builders rejected' (Matthew 21). The baser forms of alchemy, especially in the Middle Ages, took this as a sign that any particularly nasty substance would do, such as 'poudres diverse, asshes, dong, pisse, and cley' (Chaucer, *The Canon Yeoman's Tale)*, not to mention blood, hair, bones, and spittle. The more sophisticated alchemists poured scorn upon this practice and implied that the first material is not merely a common substance, which they refused to name, but a mysterious ingredient of the universe. It is

> familiar to all men, both young and old, is found in the country, in the village, in the town, in all things created by God; yet it is despised by all. Rich and poor handle it every day. It is cast into the street by servant maids. Children play with it. Yet no one prizes it, though, next to the human soul, it is the most beautiful and the most precious thing upon earth and has the power to pull down kings and princes. Nevertheless, it is esteemed the vilest and meanest of earthly things.[8]

Some authorities consider that in the early days of alchemy, the black Egyptian silt with its tremendous fertility may have provided the idea of a base substance with great nourishing and creative powers. Whether or not this is true, by the sixteenth and seventeenth centuries, the concept had become much more complex. Some writers imply that the primal material is metallic, because it is impossible to create gold from anything that does not have a metallic root; but they also hint that its form does not resemble what we usually think of as metal. And in some texts the distinction between the *prima materia* and the Stone itself, the end product of the process, is hard to define; the implication seems to be that the Stone is released from the base material by the alchemical process and is already indwelling in it when the alchemist takes it up:

> This Matter is found in one thing, out of which alone our Stone is prepared . . . without any foreign admixture; and its quality, appearance, and properties have been set forth in the following manner. It is composed of three things, yet it is only *one* . . . They also call it the universal Magnesia, or the seed of the world, from which all natural objects take their origin. Its properties are of a singular kind; for, in addition to its marvellous nature and form, it is neither hot and dry like fire, nor cold and wet like water, nor cold and dry like earth, but a perfect preparation of all the elements . . . With respect to its outward appearance, figure, form, and shape, they call it a stone, and not a stone . . . It is found *potentially* everywhere, and in everything, but in all its perfection and fullness only in *one* thing . . . By the ignorant and the beginner it is thought to be the vilest and meanest of things. It is sought by many Sages, and found by few; suspected by those that are far away, and received by those that are near; seen by all, but known by few . . .[9]

Sometimes the primal material is given special images, such as that of the toad (see p. 33). It is also associated with the Ouroboros, the circular serpent with its tail in its mouth. This goes back to the dawn of alchemy, for in an early Greek text we read:

> Here is the mystery: The serpent Ouroboros [biting his tail] is the composition which in our [work] is devoured and melted, dissolved and transformed by fermentation. It becomes dark green from which the golden colour derives. It is from this which the red comes, called the colour of cinnabar; it is the cinnabar of the philosophers. Its stomach and its back are the colour of saffron; its head is dark green, its four legs are the four imperfect metals [lead, copper, tin, iron]; its three ears are the three sublimated vapours [perhaps salt, mercury, and sulphur].
>
> The One gives to the Other its blood; and the One engenders the Other. Nature rejoices in nature; nature charms nature; nature triumphs over nature; and nature masters nature; and this is not from one nature opposing another, but through the one and same nature, through the alchemical process, with care and great effort.[10]

In *Gold Making of Cleopatra* (*c*. AD 100), the Ouroboros is drawn and the text reads: 'One is the All and by it the All and in it the All and if it does not contain the All it is nothing.' Although the later alchemists, especially in the seventeenth century, brought the philosophy of their work to the heights of sophistication, yet they still based their operations on the simplicity and unity of this premise. Transformation does not come about by mixing or combining substances. It comes primarily through purifying and perfecting the original material. This is a declaration of faith, that the divine spark dwells in every single atom that exists, however corrupt and base it may appear to our eyes.

Mercury

The alchemical serpent, or dragon, is closely connected with Mercury, the transforming agent of the alchemical process. Mercury is released and activated from the primal material, and is then transformed, fixed, and brought to perfection through the operations. Appropriately enough for such an elusive and volatile figure, alchemical descriptions of him—or her, for it is often stated that the Mercurial force is a feminine one—blend into definitions of the first material, the Stone, and 'our gold.' 'Our Mercury' is not 'common mercury,' the alchemists are quick to point out. Charles Nicholl, in *The Chemical Theatre*, grapples with these problems admirably:

> There are two directions in which alchemical Mercury leads us. On the one hand, it is a complex elaboration of chemical substance, its various qualities referring back to the properties of quicksilver, or 'common mercury' . . . But there is another direction entirely, away from chemical matter. Mercury is not, finally, a substance, or even many substances: it is a process . . . All these [alchemical writings] point to one crucial idea: that transformation is something intrinsic and contained *inside* matter . . . Each stage of this self-devouring, self-generating process bears the name 'Mercury.' Mercury, in short, is alchemy itself.

In his *Alchemical Studies*, C. G. Jung quotes from *Aurelia Occulta*, which is contained in the *Theatrum Chemicum*:

> I am the poison-dripping dragon, who is everywhere and can be cheaply had. That upon which I rest, and that which rests upon me, will be found within me by those who pursue their investigations in accordance with the rules of the Art. My water and fire destroy and put together; from my body you may extract the green lion and the red. But if you do not have exact knowledge of me, you will destroy your five senses with my fire. From my snout there comes a spreading poison that has brought death to many. Therefore you

should skilfully separate the coarse from the fine, if you do not wish to suffer utter poverty. I bestow on you the powers of the male and the female, and also those of heaven and of earth. The mysteries of my art must be handled with courage and greatness of mind if you would conquer me by the power of fire, for already very many have come to grief, their riches and labour lost. I am the egg of nature, known only to the wise . . . By the philosophers I am named Mercurius; my spouse is the [philosophic] gold; I am the old dragon, found everywhere on the globe of the earth, father and mother, young and old, very strong and very weak, death and resurrection, visible and invisible, hard and soft; I descend into the earth and ascend to the heavens, I am the highest and the lowest, the lightest and the heaviest; often the order of nature is reversed in me, as regards colour, number, weight and measure; I contain the light of nature; I am dark and light; I come forth from heaven and earth; I am known and yet do not exist at all; by virtue of the sun's rays all colours shine in me and all metals. I am the carbuncle of the sun, the most noble purified earth, through which you may change copper, iron, tin, and lead into gold.

To conclude this section on Mercury on a lighter note, I will quote from a dialogue between Mercury and an alchemist which is contained in *The New Chemical Light* by Michael Sendivogius.[11] A foolish alchemist has read that he should start his work with Mercury; he tries to heat common quicksilver, which evaporates, and so he accuses his wife of stealing it. Then he tries again, adding all sorts of substances to it such as 'herbs, urine, and vinegar' to see if he can do any better. Failing with these, he remembers reading that the dung hill is the place to seek, so he starts to use dung, but it all ends badly. Then, in a dream, a wise old man tells him to use the 'Mercury of the Sages.' He manages to conjure up Mercury in person, and tries to wrest the secret from him, but Mercury, true to form, is mischievous and avoids all the alchemist's attempts to force him into submission:

> *Alchemist:* I conjure you by the living God—are you not the Mercury of the Sages? *Mercury* (pretending to speak in a whimpering and frightened tone of voice): Master, I *am* Mercury. *Alchemist:* Why would you not obey me then? Why could I not fix you? *Mercury:* Oh, most high and mighty Master, I implore you to spare your miserable slave! I did not know that you were such a potent philosopher. *Alchemist:* Oh, could you not guess as much from the philosophical way in which I operated on you . . . (To the Mercury, in awful tones of

thunder): Now mind that you obey me, else it will be the worse for you. *Mercury:* Gladly, Master, if I can: for I am very weak. *Alchemist:* Oho, do you begin to make excuses already? *Mercury:* No, but I am very languid. *Alchemist:* What is the matter with you? *Mercury:* An Alchemist is the matter with me. *Alchemist:* Are you laughing at me, you false rogue? *Mercury:* Oh, no, no, Master, as God shall spare me, I spoke of an Alchemist—*you* are a philosopher . . . *Alchemist:* Well, I won't praise myself, but I certainly am a learned man. My wife says so too. She always calls me a profoundly learned philosopher. *Mercury:* I quite believe you. For philosophers are men whom too much learning and thought have made mad. *Alchemist:* Tell me, what am I to do with you? How am I to make you into the Philosopher's Stone? *Mercury:* Oh, my master philosopher, that I cannot tell. You are a philosopher, I am the philosopher's humble slave. Whatever he wishes to make me, I become, as far as my nature will allow. *Alchemist:* That is all very fine, but I repeat that you must tell me how to treat you, and whether you can become the Philosopher's Stone. *Mercury:* Mr. Philosopher, if you know, you can make it, and if you don't you can't . . .

Elemental Symbols

We have already looked at the basic role of the four elements in alchemy, and the qualities associated with them. Their specific functions in alchemy, however, though often obscure and mysterious, have interesting images and associations attached to them. The most important ideas concerning earth have been considered in the section on the Primal Material, but earth may also be represented by creatures such as the deer and the unicorn. Fishes are the creatures of water, birds of air, and salamanders of fire. Fire is mainly an external force in alchemy; the alchemist tends his furnace scrupulously and must apply the right degree of heat for the different stages of the operation. Often the heat is to be moderate, like that of a chicken giving warmth to her eggs. The period of gestation, after the 'seed' of the Stone has been engendered and remains in the tightly sealed vessel to come to term, is sustained by the application of fire. Often a term of forty days is mentioned for the gestation period, and this corresponds to the forty-week term for human gestation. Heat, therefore, is seen as a natural medium for growth:

> Here is our warm fire,
> Humid, lovely, and not dangerous;

That preserves all things,
And permits none to spoil.
It is even and good,
Agreeable to things to be born:
It carries everything properly heated
Away with the moisture.[12]

There are often hints that a substance undergoing transformation must yield up its secret fire, which will help to give the Stone its final power. The Salamander must be brought from his cave:

[The Salamander] is caught and pierced
So that it dies and yields up its life with its blood.
But this, too, happens for its good:
For from its blood it wins immortal life,
And then death has no more power over it.[13]

Water is closely associated with Mercury. It is the universal solvent and can also be considered as helping to give the right colour to the substance at different stages of the operation—black, white, yellow, or red. We have already seen how colour was considered to be a kind of spirit, with special properties and powers. It is also necessary to remember that all the elements were thought to have a higher form, which was quite different from that of normal earth, water, fire, and air, and it is probably these special forms which are known as 'our fire' and 'our water.' 'Our Pontic and Catholic water . . . is sweet, beautiful, clear, limpid, and brighter than gold, silver, carbuncles, or diamonds'; 'Our water is a water which does not wet the hands; it is a heavenly water, and yet not rain water'; 'Our water is serene, crystalline, pure, and beautiful.'

Sometimes 'our water' is said to be generated from the first matter; sometimes it must be added to the transforming substance to bathe it, nourish it, or colour it.

The Water of the Wise Men

When a woman mixes
Colouring with water,
She is about to wash
Linen or clothes.

The water leaves the material
When it is dried in the open air;
    But the coloured cloth
    Retains the desired colour.

Likewise the water of the wise
Penetrates all large and small metals:
    Use it
    And it tinctures things speedily.[14]

Bathing and washing were thus called 'woman's work' in alchemy. Sometimes, too, 'our water' is described as a sharp, acidic liquid capable of dissolving any gold or metal that is to be added to the mixture, and in this capacity may go under the name of the Green Dragon. Some writers on alchemy have equated this with aqua fortis or aqua regia (nitro-hydrochloric acid), acids which would certainly dissolve metal, and we do know that the alchemists had knowledge of these and other powerful chemical substances. But, again, many of the alchemists are at pains to tell us not to confuse the dissolving liquid with ordinary fluids or acids. The more practically orientated alchemists and the dabblers would have used all kinds of chemical compounds in their work; but the fact remains that in its fullest expression alchemy relied on certain specially prepared substances or elements that were considered to have properties of an extraordinary nature, not to be compared with normal preparations.

A kind of water that is given particular importance in alchemical texts is dew. A famous plate from the *Mutus Liber* (1667) shows a male and a female alchemist wringing out into a bowl dew that they have gathered by exposing large sheets of cloth to the air. Dew might be used to moisten the alchemical matter, to bathe it, or to nourish it. What would make dew so special? There are two schools of thought on this. Some alchemists, such as Armand Barbault, the twentieth-century French alchemist, consider dew to be permeated with the living vitality of the plants from which it is gathered; it thus imparts a 'green fire'—an enriching food—to the matter. Others see dew as descending from the atmosphere, the receptacle of celestial influences, the visible and fluid residue of the air, which is alive with stellar planetary energies. Both schools seem to agree that the spring quarter of the year, from the vernal equinox to the summer solstice, is the time when dew will be most potent for use.

Today's standard scientific view is that dew is a condensation of atmospheric vapour—though most modern scientists would, of course, deny that atmospheric vapour carries any special occult properties; but apparently the phenomenon is not so simple as has been supposed, and other experiments have shown that some dew may be given off from the earth.[15] Alchemists are not alone in considering dew to have particular powers. Folk tradition has long venerated it; in Britain, an old custom prevailed that maidens should go out and wash their faces in the May dew to make themselves beautiful; and in mystical traditions it also has a place. In the *Zohar* (a collection of Qabalistic writings dating from medieval times), dew is mentioned as a holy attribute:

> *v. 47*—And it is written, Isa xxvi. 19: 'The dew of the lights is thy dew.' Of the lights—that is, from the brightness of the Ancient One.
>
> *48*—And by that dew are nourished the holy supernal ones.
>
> *49*—And this is that manna which is prepared for the just in the world to come.
>
> *50*—And that dew distilleth upon the ground of the holy apple trees . . .
>
> *51*—And the appearance of this dew is white, like unto the colour of the crystal stone, whose appearance hath all colours in itself.[16]

The element of air is related to the emblem of birds, which occur in many different forms in alchemical texts. It would be possible to devote a whole book just to the symbolism of the different birds in alchemy.[17] The appearance of the *raven* or *crow* symbolizes the *nigredo,* or putrefaction of the first material. A white bird, such as the *swan,* or *dove,* may refer to the first time that the 'soul' of the matter is released, the matter having polarized into the black of the raven and the white of the more elevated bird. The *peacock* has the quality of a herald, for with the arrival of the Peacock's Tail, the show of beautiful iridescent colours in the vessel, the alchemist knows that his work is empowered and that the transformation is under way. The *pelican* is represented in connection with the legend that the pelican fed her young with the blood of her own breast, which relates to the idea that the first matter contained in itself all that it needed for transformation and perfection, including its own nourishment: this is similar to the concept of the secret 'water' being extracted from the substance and then fed back to it to help it grow. The *eagle* has a close association with Mercury, and two eagles shown fighting each other refer to the internal battle that takes place in the initial stages to untie the knot which binds the elements together. The eagle exalted or poised in the air is Mercury in his most sublime state, emblem of inspiration and knowledge, frequently a sign that the work is completed.

In *The Chymical Wedding of Christian Rosenkreutz* (1690), a long alchemical allegory concerning an initiate's quest to be accepted and present at a royal wedding, there is a description of the alchemical process in terms of a bird that emerges from an egg, changes colour and shape, and is sacrificed for its blood:

> Our Egg being now ready was taken out; But it needed no cracking, for the Bird that was in it soon freed himself, and shewed himself very jocond, yet he looked very Bloody and unshapen: . . . The Bird grew so fast under our eyes, that we well saw why the Virgin gave us such a warning of him. He bit and scratcht so devillishly about him, that could he have had his will upon any of us, he would have soon dispatched him. Now he was wholly black, and wild, wherefore other meat was brought to him . . . whereupon all his black Feathers moulted again, and instead of them there grew out Snow-white Feathers. He was somewhat tamer too, and suffered himself to be more tractable, nevertheless we did not trust him. At the third feeding his Feathers began to be so curiously coloured, that in all my Life I never saw the like colours for Beauty. He was also exceeding tame, and behaved himself so friendly with us, that (the Virgin consenting) we released him from his Captivity.

The images and symbols of alchemy helped to show the profundity of the alchemical operation. The alchemist saw his work as a great mystery, as a way of penetrating to the heart of the created world. Emblems and archetypal figures are a powerful medium for expressing the concept of a truly universal operation that reflects the basic principles of creation. The alchemist took nothing for granted; he did not treat his laboratory operations as mechanical repetitions but as a living process in which he must participate. He aimed to go beyond the realm of normal appearances and effects, to the causes of those effects, where he might glimpse 'Venus unveiled' in her chamber—an experience so intense and powerful that it was considered highly dangerous if the alchemist was not inwardly prepared. An analogous situation might be if the atomic physicist suddenly began to experience and perceive everything at the atomic level. Normal concepts of solidity, shape, and identity would cease to have meaning; it is not difficult to see that the experience could be totally overwhelming unless one was prepared and trained for it, emotionally and mentally, irrespective of how much 'atomic theory' one knew in advance.

The Celestial Influence

The relationship of the earth to the solar system and to the stars was considered very important in alchemy. In fact, until the eighteenth century, it was accepted by the majority of people that the celestial bodies were animate and possessed of particular qualities that affected life on earth. The accompanying assumption was that they were instruments, or agents of the Divine Will, and sometimes (more immediately) the tools of Nature, governing the growth of everything upon earth, including metals. The following quotation indicates the power of Nature and the part played by the planets:

> By my wisdom I govern the first principle of motion. My hands are the eighth sphere, as my Father ordained; my hammers are the seven planets with which I forge beautiful things. The substance out of which I fashion all my works, and all things under heaven, I obtain from the four elements alone . . . By my virtue and efficacy I make the imperfect perfect, whether it be a metal or a human body. I mix its ingredients, and temper the four elements. I reconcile opposites, and calm their Discord.
>
> This is the golden chain which I have linked together of my heavenly virtues and earthly substances.[18]

The earth itself was thought to be alive and sensitive to the sidereal (starry) atmosphere. The changing patterns of the planets in relation to each other and to the ecliptic (the plane of the solar system, known in astrology as the zodiac) formed a kind of celestial weather:

> The quickening power of the earth produces all things that grow forth from it, and he who says that the earth has no life makes a statement which is flatly contradicted by the most ordinary facts. For what is dead cannot produce life and growth, seeing that it is devoid of the quickening spirit. This spirit is the life and soul that dwell in the earth, and are nourished by the heavenly and sidereal

influences. For all herbs, trees, and roots, and all metals and minerals, receive their growth and nutriment from the spirit of the earth, which is the spirit of life. This spirit is itself fed by the stars, and is thereby rendered capable of imparting nutriment to all things that grow, and of nursing them as a mother does her child while it is yet in the womb.

Apart from a general 'nourishing' of the metals by the planets, a more specific effect was assumed, depending upon the exact planet involved. Each metal was said to correspond to a particular planet, and when that planet was strong in influence, the 'growth' of the metal would be accelerated within the earth. The influence could be assessed astrologically, by examining the relationship of the planets to one another and studying their position in relation to the signs of the zodiac for the time in question. The association of planets with metals was precise, and related to the active principle of the planet as defined astrologically or mythologically. Saturn, for instance, considered to be slow, profound, and weighty, had the correspondence of lead, the heaviest of the metals concerned. Venus, planet of ease, pleasure, beauty, and malleability, corresponded to copper, a soft and gleaming metal. The sun corresponded to gold, the moon to silver, Mercury to quicksilver, Mars to iron, and Jupiter to tin. The alchemist would need to know and understand these correspondences well, since it was common to try and prepare elixirs of the other metals apart from silver and gold, especially as medicinal remedies. Often in the alchemical texts one will find the metals called by the names of the planets themselves.

Since Nature was said to operate through the medium of the planets, the alchemist, seeking to use art to accelerate and perfect the natural processes, must understand and utilize the principles of stellar influences. Many alchemists, therefore, were skilled astrologers. Astrology is the art of interpreting the planetary positions as they relate to the earth, by mapping them (drawing up a horoscope) and judging what this map will mean in terms of human affairs or natural processes. Such a map can be drawn for a time past, present, or future. In alchemy it was common to select in advance a favourable time astrologically to begin the Great Work, and the initiation of new stages of the process might also be governed by astrological conditions. A general rule was that the work was best begun at or around the vernal equinox, when the sun moves into the sign of Aries, the first point of the zodiac. However, more elaborate calculations and assessments were frequently employed, just as a gardener might have it in mind to sow certain seeds in a particular week, but would vary the timing according to prevalent weather and ground conditions.

One's personal horoscope would also be taken into account, and indeed it was a tenet of early Chinese alchemy that a suitable birth chart was a prerequisite for a successful alchemist. Astrology, like alchemy, is not a dogmatic tradition; it is based on old and well-tried principles but relies on the skill, judgement, and integrity of the practitioner to achieve good results. Like alchemy, it can become debased and superstitious when used without understanding, and in certain alchemical texts astrological indications are given out like magical formulae. In *The Testament of Cremer*, for instance, we come across the following assertions: 'About the fifteenth day of March take three oz. of quicksilver . . . in October you should fill a water-tight box . . . with fresh horse dung, and thrust your glass vessel into it . . . Never look at the mixture but at the time of the full moon.' The more precise the instructions in alchemical manuscripts, the more we may suspect that they are derivative texts, handing on what are believed to be recipes for success with no grasp of the principles involved.

Alchemists perpetuated the view that the cosmos is whole and alive and that all its components have spirit and purpose; the stars and the planets provide a 'field' of energy that man can either experience passively or use actively for creative purposes. The alchemist therefore cannot work against the natural and stellar influences, but he can channel them to bring about transformation:

> Let me sum up in a few words what I have to say. The substance is of heavenly birth, its life is preserved by the stars, and nourished by the four elements; then it must perish, and be putrefied; again, by the influence of the stars, which works through the elements, it is restored to life, and becomes once more a heavenly thing that has its habitation in the highest region of the firmament. Then you will find that the heavenly has assumed an earthly body, and that the earthly body has been reduced to a heavenly substance.[19]

THE ALCHEMIST
IMAGE AND REALITY

What image does the word alchemist conjure up? Perhaps that of a lean and bearded figure, dressed in a dark and dusty cloak, muttering mysterious incantations as he leans over his cauldrons and bubbling retorts. When the history of alchemy is thoroughly studied, it soon becomes obvious that this picture is far from the truth, but it must also be noted that even in its heyday alchemy was considered a subject for ridicule. The majority of people were not well informed about alchemical aims and practices, partly because most serious alchemists kept very much to themselves, and those who did pronounce themselves publicly to be alchemists were often the most fraudulent or foolish practitioners of all. It is from their absurd and extreme activities that the popular image of alchemy derives.

> Their clothes be bawdy and worn thread-bare,
> Men may smell them for multipliers where they go;
> To file their fingers with corrosives they do not spare
> Their eyes be bleryd, and their cheeks both lean and blue ...
> They search for the stone in soot, dung, urine, wine, blood, eggs.
> To see their houses it is a noble sport,
> What furnaces, what glasses there be of divers shape;
> What salts, what powders, what oils, and waters fort,
> How eloquently, *de materia prima,* they clape,
> And yet to find the truth they have no hap.[1]

Many came to ruin through their search for the stone, addicted to the quest for gold and spending all their time and money in fruitless experiment. Chaucer illustrated such a plight in *The Canon Yeoman's Tale*, where the yeoman reveals sadly:

> With this chanoun I dwelt have seven yeer,
> And of his science am I never the neer.

Al that I hadde, I have y-lost ther-by;
And god wot, so hath many mo than I.
Ther I was wont to be right fresh and gay
Of clothing and of other good array,
Now may I were an hose upon myn head;
And wher my colour was bothe fresh and reed,
Now is it wan and of a leden hewe;
Who-so it useth, sore shal he rewe.
And of my swink yet blered is myn yë,
Lo! which advantage is to multiplye!
That slyding science hath me maad so bare,
That I have no good, wher that ever I fare;
And yet I am endetted so ther-by
Of gold that I have borwed, trewely,
That whyl I live, I shall it quyte never.
Lat every man be war by me for ever!

The unsuccessful experimenters were characterized by a stink of brimstone, worn-out clothes, an unhealthy tinge to the skin, and a general air of poverty. The charlatans could he distinguished by their bragging and boasting, their readiness to talk about the art of alchemy, and their willingness to promise spectacular transmutations; they often lived a wandering life—presumably because when they became too well known in one place they would have to move on fast!

Going beyond the superficial picture, though, we find quite different types of people seriously involved in the study of alchemy. In medieval times these were often monks, but both then and later the aspirants included noblemen, men of business, men of learning—and a few women. All had to have enough time and money to support their researches, for there were likely to be months and even years of long experiment, and the alchemist had to be committed to regulating the fire, mixing, adding, and, above all, to waiting and watching for the right reactions in the vessel.

In medieval times the monastic environment provided excellent opportunities for alchemical work. Monasteries were natural centres of learning, since all books were written in manuscript form and one of the chief occupations of monks was in copying out and illuminating the texts. Many monasteries had fine libraries and received visitors from afar, bringing new insights and theories from other teachers and countries. And of course monks, free from domestic responsibilities, had time to pursue their private researches.

We find many traces of monastic alchemists. In Elias Ashmole's anthology of alchemical poetry *(Theatrum Chemicum Britannicum)*, we find a contribution from the rather sinister-sounding 'Pearce, the Black Monk,' who had a fair talent for verse, the style of which would seem to place him in the medieval period:

> I am Mercury the mighty flower,
> I am most worthy of honour;
> I am source of Sol, Luna and Mars,
> I am settler of Saturn, and source of Venus,
> I am Empress, Princess, and Regal of Queens,
> I am Mother of Mirror, and maker of light,
> I am head and highest and fairest in sight . . .[2]

Often the story of ecclesiastical alchemists is known only when there is some unusual or scandalous biographical detail that has caused them to be remembered. Lynn Thorndike quotes **John of Rupescissia** as an example of a Franciscan monk involved in alchemy. He was a Catalan living in the fourteenth century and had studied philosophy at Toulouse before entering the order. However, he appears to have committed some misdemeanour, for he was imprisoned for some time in the local convent. This did not deter him from continuing to write, and during these and later years, he wrote books of prophecies and of alchemy. One, entitled *The Book of the Service of Philosophy,* was extensively copied and circulated. He dealt chiefly with the distillation of an elixir that would prolong youth and health.

John Dastin is remembered for his courageous fight to keep the name of alchemy untarnished. He was a member of an austere order and lived in the first half of the fourteenth century.

Pope John XXII had condemned alchemy because of the proliferation of fraudulent practitioners. He passed an edict by which those caught counterfeiting gold and silver had to repay the equivalent sum of money back into the common treasury; persistent cases were to have their goods confiscated and be branded as criminals: offending clerics were to be deprived of their livings. Dastin wrote both to the Pope and to Cardinal

Orsini assuring them that there was more to alchemy than deception, and maintained that it was within the possibilities of nature to prepare the alchemical elixir. He wrote in detail, describing the complexities to such a degree that perhaps the Pope was dazzled by such erudition. At any rate, Dastin does not seem to have suffered for his efforts; indeed E. J. Holmyard tells us that when the Pope died, he left an enormous fortune that was reputed to be of alchemical origin!

The most famous alchemical monk is **Sir George Ripley**, who came of an aristocratic family and was a Canon regular in the Augustinian priory at Bridlington, in Yorkshire. This priory had a strong tradition of learning, and in the fifteenth century Ripley made it the base for his alchemical experiments, apparently antagonizing the other inhabitants by the smells and fumes that were generated in his laboratory. One interesting feature of Ripley's alchemical education is that he spent some time in Rhodes, as a guest of the Knights of St. John of Jerusalem. Rhodes had been occupied by the Knights since 1310 and quickly gained a reputation for being a cosmopolitan centre of learning, a little like a latter-day Alexandria. The Knights' community, though based on Catholic principles, was receptive to innovative ideas that would have been suspect elsewhere, and many came to Rhodes to teach and learn in an atmosphere of comparative intellectual freedom.

Since one of the chief occupations of the Knights of St. John was healing the sick, there was a natural connection between their endeavours to promote the study of medicine and herbalism, and alchemy, whose Elixir had the reputation of being a panacea. In the late medieval period, Jacques Millac, a French herbalist and apothecary who had antagonized the Catholic Church in his own country because of his interest in alchemy, joined the Order in order to be able to live in Rhodes and experiment as he wished. A university had been established there that was noted for its teaching of medicine, while a special school for apothecaries was attached to the hospital run by the Knights. Ripley (in the fifteenth century) is understood to have gained at least some of his alchemical expertise during his stay on Rhodes. Another noted alchemist, **Bernard of Treves** (probably in the fourteenth century), completed his alchemical studies on Rhodes, where it is said that he met a 'man of religion' whose alchemical library was attractive enough to Bernard to keep him there for eight years, teaching him what a lifetime of experiment had failed to do.

Ripley became well known for such works as *The Compound of Alchemy* (containing the famous passage on the Twelve Gates), which quickly became established as alchemical classics. With Ripley, a link is formed between the clerical and the secular alchemist, for **Thomas Norton**, a well-to-do Bristol merchant, claimed that Ripley was his teacher. Norton, who may also have held the post of privy councillor to Edward IV, published his work *The Ordinall of Alchemy* anonymously in 1477. However, despite the appearance of discretion and modesty, he plainly had hopes that someone would recognize his hand in the work, as he concealed his name in an easy cipher which revealed the motto:

Thomas Norton of Briseto
A parfet Master ye maie him trowe.

Thomas Charnock, born around 1524, was also taught alchemy by monks. His profession is not known and he had little education, though this did not deter him from the search. His own account of his work makes fine and amusing reading because of the zest and frankness with which he writes. He was plainly pleased with his own verse. He recounts how, when in search of alchemical knowledge, he chanced to meet a blind friar who tells him, not knowing Charnock's identity, that he will only teach the art to a most gifted and wonderful young man that he has heard of called Charnock! His virtues are apparently such that:

Wherefore his knowledge, gravity and wit,
He may well be crowned Poet Laureate.

Charnock suffered several setbacks in his alchemical work. The most infuriating came when he was called up to fight at Calais:

When I saw there was none other boot
But that I must go spite of my heart took root;
In my fury I took a hatchet in my hand,
And brake all my work whereas it did stand,
And as for my pots I knocked them together,
And also my glasses into many a shiver . . .

From the sixteenth century onwards, alchemy became a magnet for men of learning, especially those seeking a comprehensive knowledge of the universe. Their creed was that there should be no boundaries between arts, sciences, mysticism, and occult knowledge. Each discipline was seen as a valid way both of gaining knowledge about the created world and of learning to operate within it. A metaphysical understanding would both help to explain physical phenomena and inspire practical inventions. Yet, though alchemy was taken seriously by those of considerable intellectual reputation, it certainly never found universal favour. Some were simply sceptical of alchemical claims, but others saw in alchemy and occult arts the machinations of the devil.

Examples of this last attitude can seem amusing to us nowadays. **John Dee** (1527-1608), a controversial Elizabethan figure, was suspected of being a sorcerer when he invented an elaborate mechanical beetle for a stage play that gave the illusion of flying! Dee was a remarkable man who took a keen interest in alchemy; in later life he had laboratories built at his house in Mortlake. He became the object of a great deal of fear and suspicion, but he was always a favourite of Queen Elizabeth, who consulted him as to a suitable astrological date and time for her coronation. He was well versed in mechanics, optics, navigation, history, and mathematics and was farsighted enough to propose a national scheme for the preservation of ancient monuments and a national 'Library Royal.'

Dee took a special interest in clairvoyance and is often remembered for his association with the dubious Edward Kelley, who acted as a scryer for him in his attempts to communicate with the world of spirits and angels. But, Dee was not the unquestioning dupe that some authorities have assumed, for his diaries show that he was often critical of Kelley. However, he found certain qualities or psychic abilities in Kelley that he valued, and together they tried both crystal gazing and dowsing for hidden treasure.

Any assessment of Dee as a man has to be tempered by one's own views. If it is considered that the idea of angels or spirits is a delusion, then one is obliged to condemn Dee as a man of enormous intelligence and skill who was unfortunately prone to fantasy. If the gaining of knowledge through 'angelic' beings is considered possible, then the picture of Dee becomes that of a man who developed his inner resources as well as his outer abilities, making mistakes, perhaps, but nevertheless a man of integrity.

Dee and Kelley went to Poland together, where they undertook to demonstrate alchemical transformation to the Emperor of Bohemia; but the attempt failed and they were dismissed in a state of near poverty. Dee and Kelley then parted company, with Kelley devoting himself to alchemy, and Dee becoming Warden of Christ's College, Manchester. Dee was never happy thereafter, especially after the death of Queen Elizabeth, for James I showed himself most unsympathetic to any activities associated with magic or alchemy.

In the sixteenth and seventeenth centuries, an interest in alchemy was apparent in the highest circles in both England and Scotland. As Adam McLean writes:

> Now at that time in Scotland there was quite a flourishing alchemical school probably centred around Napier, including the Earl of Argyle, perhaps William Drummond of Hawthornden the poet, Patrick Ruthven (who was at the time imprisoned in the Tower of London and was part of the Tower Group of Alchemists which included the Earl of Northumberland, Henry Percy, Sir Walter Raleigh, and Thomas Hariot). Another important Scottish alchemist of the period was Sir George Erskine, who was very close to King James . . . Sir George Erskine's alchemical manuscripts, a large part of which still survive, indicate his broad reading in the alchemical tradition, there being scarcely an important alchemical work that is not included in his collections.[3]

John Napier (1550-1617), better known as the inventor of logarithms, was a serious student of alchemy who was instructed and helped by a German alchemist, **Daniel Müller**. Müller had a great influence upon the Scottish school of alchemists, and some of the letters he wrote explaining the alchemical process in allegorical terms still survive. For instance, a copy of a letter sent to the Earl of Argyle begins:

> Right Honourable,
>
> Your earnest desire to profit in this study of metaphysical philosophy, I thought it good to give your Lordship a taste of such marrow as I have by God's assistance sucked out of the bones of old philosophy . . .

He describes the alchemical work as needing the living blood of 'a most ugly, venomous, and horrid flying dragon' who dwells in 'the hidden caverns of one huge Mountain.' (This is probably a reference to the powerful and volatile Mercury concealed in an unpleasant substance of metallic origin.) As is often the case, the appearance of such an alchemical adept upon the scene is mysterious; we do not know whether Müller was sent for, or whether he came of his own volition; nor do we know who his associates were in Germany.

Many accounts of the lives of alchemists have been passed down without proper investigation, and undoubtedly several of them are distortions of the truth or even complete inventions. *The Testament of Cremer* claims to be the story of an Abbot Cremer of Westminster, who was instructed in alchemy by Ramon Lull. Cremer introduces Lull to the King (Edward III) and Lull promises to make gold for the King if the King himself will go to war against the Turks and use some of the gold for enriching a monastic house. The gold was duly made, it is said, but the king broke his promise, leaving 'that holy man sore afflicted in spirit.' However, no record exists of any Abbot Cremer, there is no proof that Lull was an alchemist, and the 'rose nobles,' coins said to have been struck from the alchemical gold, are anachronisms.

Occasionally a legend can actually devalue the work of an alchemist, as in the case of **Michael Sendivogius** (1566–1636). For a long time it has been stated that Sendivogius was not a genuine alchemical adept, but that he came into possession of the 'Stone' in a powder form via his involvement with Alexander Seton, a Scot. Seton was an exhibitionist who, it is said, gave various public transformations of metal into gold and wandered throughout Europe making a reputation for himself as a kind of alchemical conjuror who was willing to produce gold, but would never stay long enough to impart the secret to anyone. Eventually his luck ran out; the Elector of Saxony tortured him and threw him into jail when he refused to say how the operation was done. The story goes that Sendivogius, a Moravian, was at that time a keen but unsuccessful student of alchemy, and hearing of Seton's imprisonment laid successful plans to free him. After a dramatic flight to Cracow, Seton finally gave Sendivogius some of the supreme powder, but, again, would not tell him the secret of its manufacture. Sendivogius was then able to perform transmutations but could not make the Stone himself; it is said that he married Seton's widow with an eye to stepping into Seton's alchemical shoes, but this produced no helpful results. In pique, he circulated Seton's manuscripts as his own work.

Careful research by both Professor Hubicki and Professor Bugaj has shown that this story is a fabrication, probably invented in the seventeenth century by a Frenchman, Pierre Des Noyers, who had a dislike of Poles in general and of Sendivogius in particular. It has been perpetuated in various histories of alchemy until the present day. But Sendivogius can be affirmed as the true author of works ascribed to him; further, one only has to read a text such as *A New Chemical Light* to realize that he is a writer of considerable maturity and depth. His work is thoughtful, lucid, structured, and philosophical. His explanations of cosmic hierarchy and natural processes are worth reading in their own right, whether or not one is interested in alchemy. It would be impossible to judge this man as a semi-imposter who had no real alchemical knowledge, and indeed alchemists of his day such as Michael Maier and Sir Isaac Newton admired Sendivogius and regarded him as one of the greatest masters of the art.

The evidence now suggests that Sendivogius was a highly educated man who probably came to know Seton at the University of Altdorf and may even have given *him* some alchemical instruction. He worked at his art in Prague, which was famous for its alchemists, became councillor to Rudolph II, and was also respected as a healer and a diplomat. He may well have helped Seton escape from prison, but he never married his widow.[4]

Women in Alchemy

Women have played a less prominent part in alchemy than men. Plainly, the demands of an art that required constant and prolonged attention made it impossible for most women to pursue it seriously, for it would not fit in easily with childbearing or with the running of a household. However, certain women alchemists are known to have existed; some husbands and wives worked together, and it is possible that further research would bring to light accounts of more women who were interested in alchemy. We have already seen that Maria the Jewess was a noted alchemist of antiquity, although we know nothing about her life. She was esteemed as an adept and probably gathered a school of alchemists around her. Likewise, from the same period comes the more mysterious Kleopatra, whose name as an author of alchemical treatises may simply have been borrowed from the Egyptian Queen of that name, or who may have been a real alchemist of some influence. Zosimos, the Greek alchemist, had a sister called Theosebeia who was involved in alchemy, but we know of her existence only through fragments of letters that Zosimos wrote to her. Later times have no well-known lady alchemists on record, but it is possible that they were overlooked both by historians and contemporary alchemists. There are a few brief references: John Aubrey (the seventeenth-century historian) mentions that Mary Sidney (the wife of the Earl of Pembroke) was 'a great chymist, and spent yearly a great deale in that study.' Lady Anne Conway (1642-1684) has already been cited as being highly influential in the Rosicrucian circle of the period, whose members would have included alchemy as one of their chief studies.

A theme shadowy to unravel, but in some ways more interesting to contemplate, is that of a man and woman working together in 'the Great Work.' The process of alchemy depends upon correct understanding of the male and female principles inherent in matter (sulphur and mercury), of separating them and uniting them in harmony, and it is therefore readily understandable that the alchemists would have sought to echo this idea in their own work. In certain pictures, autobiographical writings, and accounts, we find the idea that both the man and the woman had something vital to contribute to the operation. Illustrations in the *LiberMutus* (1677) show a man and a woman working together to gather dew, tend the vessel and the furnace, and assist each other in almost every stage of the process. The illustrations show precisely the different actions performed by each one of the pair, giving an impression of work that is ritualized and in which male and female must perform their tasks in a clearly defined and complementary manner. In one illustration, they kneel on each side of the furnace; the man has his hands folded and his head bowed in prayer while the woman gazes upwards, lifting one arm high in a graceful gesture of blessing. Armand Barbault, a noted twentieth-century alchemist, always worked in conjunction with a female partner and has this to say about the role of the man and the woman in the operation:

> Through her extreme sensibility and the mobility of her own bodily fluids, the woman is to a certain extent in a favourable position to cross to higher levels and so receive instructions for her partner. His role, on the other hand, is far more earth-bound. He constructs the work on the material plane, at which level the woman stays in the background. She stands, therefore, on the right-hand side of the arcana, the 'passive side,' the side of the psyche.[5]

Sometimes it is implied that while the man may experiment and labour over his retorts and materials, the woman is needed to add the right touch to bring the work to life. There is an example of this in an early Chinese text:

> A gentleman of the Yellow Gate at the Han [imperial court], Cheng Wei, loved the art of the Yellow and White [alchemy]. He took a wife and secured a girl from a household which knew recipes ... [he tried to] make gold in accordance with 'The Great Treasure' in the pillow [of the King of Huai-nan, but] it would not come. His wife however came and watched ... Wei was then fanning the ashes to heat the

bottle. In the bottle there was quicksilver. His wife said, 'I want to try and show you something.' She thereupon took a drug out of a bag and threw a very little into [the retort]. It was absorbed and in a short while she turned out [the contents of the retort]. It had already become silver. Wei was greatly astonished and said, 'The way of [alchemy] was near and was possessed by you. But why did you not tell me sooner?' His wife replied, 'In order to get it, it is necessary for one to have the [proper] fate.'[6]

Both Helvetius and Nicolas Flamel, whom we shall meet towards the end of this chapter, worked in close collaboration with their wives. In the case of Helvetius, his wife spurred him on to experiment with the powdered stone he had been given when he himself despaired of any success in the matter: 'Late that night my wife (who was a most curious student and enquirer after the art) came soliciting and vexing me to make experiment of that little spark . . . saying to me, unless this be done, I shall have no rest nor sleep all this night.' Flamel, throughout the long years of his search, was dependent upon the help and encouragement of his wife Perenelle. Together they performed the perfect alchemical transmutation, and Flamel was more than ready to acknowledge Perenelle's essential contribution: 'I may speak it with truth, I have made it three times, with the help of Perenelle, who understood it as well as I because she helped me with my operations, and without doubt, if she would have enterprised to have done it alone, she had attained the end and perfection thereof.'[7]

In all, it has to be said that alchemy was practised primarily by men, but it was not forbidden in any way to women, and it is likely that there were many women alchemists—certainly many working with their husbands—whose endeavours have passed unrecorded in history.

Laboratories and Their Inhabitants:
Mistakes and Disasters

It is not the intention of this book to examine in any great detail the range of alchemical equipment and substances used, but it is interesting to take a brief look at the day-to-day running of the laboratory and at the accidents and troubles that caused the alchemists much grief and their enemies mirth. Contemporary paintings often show the laboratory as a busy place, and one may be surprised to see a number of workers stoking, pounding, pouring, and so on. Not all alchemists worked this way; in fact, using assistants is in some ways contrary to the spirit of alchemy, which demands the total involvement of the practitioner rather than the delegation of work. However, the practical demands of a temperamental furnace needing to be kept at constant heat and of pots that must be watched lest they boil made the keeping of servants necessary for many. Thomas Norton decreed that eight in all would be ideal, but those of lesser fortunes might manage with four—two on duty and two that 'sleepeth or goeth to Kerke.' He also recommended that the alchemist should consult his own horoscope, especially the sixth house, to see how best to manage his servants.

The athanor (furnace) seems to have been freestanding, brick built, and about three feet in height with a conical cover on the top that could be taken off to allow a vessel to be placed in the chamber above the fire itself. Because pottery and glass vessels were needed, one of the great problems was breakages, especially at high temperatures. Thomas Charnock discusses the difficulties of ordering vessels, when the design must be made explicit to the potter or the glassmaker without letting him know that it is intended for alchemical use. (Many alchemists kept their work entirely secret for fear of public antagonism.) He advises telling the potter that the wares are needed to distil water to treat blindness; making the tabernacle (or support for the vessel) needs the co-operation of a joiner, who can be told that it is a burrow for a fox!

Charnock had first-hand experience of laboratory catastrophe:

Yet one thing of truth I weill thee tell,
What greate mishap unto my worke befell;
It was upon a New Yeare's Day at noon,
My tabernacle caught fire, it was soon done:
For within an hour it was right well,
And straight of fire I had a smell.
I ran up to my work right,
And when I came it was on a fire light:
Then was I in such fear that I began to stagger,
As if I had been wounded to the heart with a dagger;
And can you blame me? no I think not much,
For if I had been a man anything rich,
I had rather have given 100 Marks to the Poor,
Rather than that hap should have chanced that hour.
For I was well onward of my work truly.

Explosions and poisonings being well-known hazards of the alchemical laboratory, it is little wonder that the alchemical quest was thought of as a dangerous one, since it could consume a man's health and wealth. The constant effort and devotion alchemy demanded could easily turn to obsessive mania. Bernard of Treves and Godfrey Leporis (fourteenth century), for instance, spent ten years in unsuccessful experiment, using over 2,000 hens' eggs in one project. Bernard only desisted when he was rendered unconscious by the fumes of vitriol for fourteen months. When he recovered he sold all his estate to pay off his debts, and then took up alchemy again.

Some texts, such as *The Sophic Hydrolith*, give guidance so that the alchemist may judge when matters are not progressing satisfactorily. Premature redness, lack of coagulation, and so on are 'symptoms of a false composition and temperature, or of some kind or other of carelessness.' The author continues: 'If these defects are not immediately seen to, they will speedily become incorrigible. A cunning adept should be acquainted with the various devices by which they may be remedied; and I will recount them here for the sake of the beginner . . .' A far worse fate is promised by an early Chinese writer, should the student go astray:

> Gases from food consumed will make noises inside the intestines and stomach. The right essence will be exhaled and the evil one inhaled. Days and nights will be passed without sleep, moon after moon. The body will then be tired out, giving rise to an appearance of insanity. The hundred pulses will stir and boil so violently as to drive away peace of mind and body . . . Ghostly things will make their appearance, at which he will marvel even in his sleep. He is then led to rejoice, thinking that he is assured of longevity. But all of a sudden he is seized by an untimely death.[8]

It could be dangerous to let the world at large know that you practised alchemy: if people associated alchemy with the devil, they might hang you; if they thought you possessed a secret for making gold they would pursue you greedily: with kings and potentates, it was often a case of 'prove it or die.' Sometimes laws were passed forbidding the practice of alchemy, or else insisting that a special licence be obtained if the alchemist could prove himself to be a genuine seeker. The anonymous author of *An Open Entrance to the Shut Palace of the King* paints a most pathetic picture of the alchemists' lot:

So long as the secret is possessed by a comparatively small number of philosophers, their lot is anything but a bright and happy
one; surrounded as we are on every side by the cruel greed and
the prying suspicion of the multitude, we are doomed, like Cain, to
wander over the earth homeless and friendless. Not for us are the
soothing influences of domestic happiness; not for us the delightful
confidences of friendship. Men who covet our golden secret pursue
us from place to place, and fear closes our lips, when love tempts
us to open ourselves freely to a brother. Thus we feel prompted at
times to burst forth into the desolate exclamation of Cain: 'Whoever finds me will slay me.' Yet we are not the murderers of our
brethren; we are anxious only to do good to our fellow-men. But
even our kindness and charitable compassion are rewarded with
black ingratitude—ingratitude that cries to heaven for vengeance.
It was only a short time ago that, after visiting the plague-stricken
haunts of a certain city, and restoring the sick to perfect health by
means of my miraculous medicine, I found myself surrounded by
a yelling mob, who demanded that I should give to them my Elixir
of the Sages; and it was only by changing my dress and my name,
by shaving off my beard and putting on a wig, that I was enabled
to save my life . . .

Learning and Teaching

Some kindly advice to the alchemical novice is given in the treatise as
follows:

In the first place, let him carry on his operations with great secrecy
in order that no scornful or scurrilous person may know of them; for
nothing discourages the beginner so much as the mockery, taunts
and well-meant advice of foolish outsiders. Moreover, if he does
not succeed, secrecy will save him from derision; if he does succeed, it will safeguard him against the persecution of greedy and
cruel tyrants. In the second place, he who would succeed in the
study of this Art should be persevering, industrious, learned, gentle,
good-tempered, a close student, and neither easily discouraged nor
slothful; he may work in co-operation with one friend, not more,
but should be able to keep his own counsel; it is also necessary that
he should have a little capital to procure the necessary implements,
etc, and to provide himself with food and clothing while he follows
this study, so that his mind may be undistracted by care and anxi-
ety. Above all, let him be honest, God-fearing, prayerful and holy.
Being thus equipped, he should study Nature, read the books of the

genuine Sages, who are neither imposters nor jealous churls, and study them day and night . . .[9]

Many would-be alchemists tried to learn the secrets of the art through books and manuscripts available to them. These could produce an alternating frenzy of hope and despair as work after work was studied and then cast aside with the riddle still unsolved. One frank account, quoted by Holmyard, comes from Denis Zachaire, a French alchemist of the sixteenth century:

> There [in Paris in 1546] for ten crowns I bought books of philosophy, ancient as well as modern, part of which were printed while others were written by hand . . . And having hired for myself a small room in the Faubourg Saint-Marceau, I lived there for a year, with a small boy who served me, without frequenting anyone, studying day and night on those authors, with the result that at the end of a month I made one conclusion, then another, then I changed it almost entirely. So, while waiting for a conclusion in which there was not variety nor contradiction between the sentences of the books of the philosophers, I spent an entire year and part of another without being able to gain over my study to the extent of being able to make any entire and perfect conclusion.

It was the convention in alchemical writing for each author to slip in a hint that no work had ever been so bold, so explicit, so ready to give away cherished secrets, such as the following, ascribed to Edward Kelley:

> Many books may'st thou see
> That is not writ so openly.
> Therefore I pray you for charity,
> To keep this book very secretly.

Such a statement was usually followed by a condemnation of all the wicked lies that had been passed off as alchemical truths in other books:

> When I considered in my mind the great number of deceitful books and forged Alchemistic 'receipts,' which have been put into circulation by heartless imposters, though they do not contain even a spark of truth—and how many persons have been and are still daily led astray by them?—it occurred to me that I could not do better than

communicate the Talent committed to me by the Father of Light to the Sons and Heirs of Knowledge.[10]

Often the reader is lured on with promises of frank revelations. But time and time again this is not to be; the author slips in an apology for not going any further, but indicates that he has already said more than he should, and fears to break his vow if he continues: 'But if the complement is concealed let not the son of learning wonder. For we have not concealed it from him, but have delivered it in such a speech, as it must necessarily be hid from the evil, and unjust, and the unwise cannot discern it.'[11]

The message of the written texts seems to be: Let those who understand already understand what I have written; let those who are ignorant remain ignorant. (How one could banish ignorance and gain understanding through the words and symbols alone is left something of a mystery.) The anonymous author of *The Hunting of the Green Lion* makes a virtue out of this in his greeting to his readers:

All hail to the noble company
Of true students in holy alchemy,
Whose noble practice does them teach
To veil their secrets with misty speech . . .[12]

Although some students claimed to have mastered alchemical practice through books, most needed a more direct contact with the tradition. Over and over, again alchemists emphasize the fact that if the mystery is not revealed directly through a dream or vision, then it must come from 'living Masters.' Thomas Norton tells us that 'it must needs be taught from mouth to mouth,' and that not even one's own children are entitled to learn it. He himself says that his master (George Ripley) tested his sincerity in various ways, one of which was by requiring him to ride a hundred miles in each direction to spend a forty-day training period with his teacher. Students are advised against wasting their money on tuition from any vain boaster who claims to be skilled in alchemy. Only those who know nothing, it is said, talk freely. If you are offered instruction:

Spend not thy money away in waste,
Give not to every speech credence;
But first examine, grope and taste;

And as thou provest, so put thy confidence,
And ever beware of great expense . . .
One thing, one glass, one furnace and no more,
Behold this principle if he take,
And if he do not, then let him go . . .[13]

Sometimes it is indicated that a master could take only one pupil to instruct, and that the master should choose the pupil, rather than vice versa. The suitability of the initiate was emphasized as early as the second century AD, in the Chinese alchemical text by Go (Ko) Hung, who said: 'The adept must moreover learn the method directly from those skilled in the art. Books are inadequate. What is written in books is only enough for beginners. The rest is kept secret and is given only in oral teaching. Worship of the proper gods is necessary. The art can moreover only be learned by those who are specially blessed. People are born under suitable or unsuitable stars. Above all, belief is necessary. Disbelief brings failure.'[14] This echoes the theme that success is never guaranteed in alchemy. Correct conditions are essential, and this includes a correct mental attitude.

Some of the stories concerning the initiation of alchemists are fascinating, but even apparently factual narratives may be to some extent allegorical. Historians are generally pleased to quote the testimony of **Helvetius** (Johann Friedrich Schweitzer), for this appears to be a straightforward account of a meeting between Helvetius and an alchemical adept. The story, in brief, which is recounted in *The Golden Calf,* is that on 27 December 1666 a stranger appeared at Helvetius' house in the Hague and showed him some pieces of matter, 'each about the bigness of a small walnut, transparent, of a pale brimstone colour,' which the stranger said was the Philosopher's Stone. He refused to give Helvetius any of it, but talked to him about how he could turn stones into gems, produce healing medicines, and make 'a limpid clear water sweeter than honey' (probably the famed Mercurial water). He showed Helvetius some golden medals that had been struck from alchemical gold. Three weeks later, he returned and, after much pleading from Helvetius, gave him a tiny 'crumb' of the stone. When Helvetius doubted that such a small amount could do anything at all, the stranger took it back, threw half of it into the fire, and gave him back the rest. He instructed him in the art of preparing the stone, telling him that only two substances in all are necessary, and that the work is carried out in one crucible and is neither lengthy nor expensive if correctly understood. He did not return again, but Helvetius, with the assistance of his wife, performed a successful transmutation with the stone, and the gold which was produced was publicly assayed and found to be of excellent quality.

Some scholars have found this story difficult to assess, for on the one hand Helvetius was a respected physician and botanical writer, not given to deliberate deception; yet on the other, the tale of marvellous gold produced in this way seems to them to have little credibility. I would suggest that much of the tale is likely to be allegory, not because Helvetius wanted to boast and lie about his alchemical powers, but because he wanted to teach certain facts about alchemical training through a medium that is at least part allegorical. We have already seen that allegory and symbol were standard features of alchemical communication. When this account is examined in detail, certain aspects can be viewed in this light.

The stranger who mysteriously arrives is described as wearing 'a plebeian habit, honest Gravity, and serious authority; of a mean stature, a little long face, with a few small pock holes, and most black hair, not at all curled, a beardless chin, about three or four and forty years of age (as I guessed).' Such a description is a perfect portrait of Saturn personified. The astrological attributes of Saturn (as we have seen, alchemists were well-versed in planetary lore) when applied to human appearance are leanness, dark hair and complexion, a lowliness of clothing and height, and a serious manner. Saturn, additionally, was sometimes depicted as the wise guide and instructor in alchemy, who could lead the initiate to understanding. Even the anecdotal detail that the stranger forgot to wipe the snow and mud off his boots when entering Helvetius' nicely furnished room has a significance in this context, for Saturn is the planet of dirt and earth, and those under his influence are said to be somewhat grubby in their own manners and appearance.

And what of Helvetius himself, as he portrays his reactions? His behaviour is just like that of Mercury, the agent of alchemy—ever-questioning, arguing, even trying to steal the Stone at one point. Mercury is the natural active force of alchemy; in its primal state it is volatile and unreliable and must be disturbed, released, and then fixed in a higher state in order to bring about the transformation.

Studied carefully, this text may yield up a wealth of information as to *how* alchemy can be learnt, and it perhaps implies that the process of initiation is similar to the process of creating the Stone itself. A clever man such as Helvetius is quite capable of weaving his knowledge of alchemical training into a kind of parable, which contains much information and truth but not in a literal fashion. Indeed, it is much more likely that he would do this than that he would openly describe his training, since it was normal for this to be kept secret.

Nicolas Flamel, who lived in the fourteenth century, leaves us another account of his discovery of alchemy. This may perhaps be a more straightforward narrative, but we cannot be certain. Flamel, a notary living in Paris, dreamed of a wonderfully illustrated book, which he later actually came across and purchased. It seemed to be made out of 'delicate rinds ... of tender young trees.' It was covered in brass and inscribed with strange characters; it contained twenty-one leaves and was 'full of fair figures,' such as Mercury, a virgin swallowed by serpents, a crucified serpent (the slain mercury that has to be resurrected), and a mountain with a 'fair flower' on the top (probably the metallic seed of the First Substance). Flamel and his wife Perenelle, whom he had lately married in middle age, pored over this together after he had spent many solitary hours trying to unravel its secrets, and although she could not understand it any better than he, yet Flamel found it a great comfort to study it with her. He had the emblems painted in his house, and he consulted some of the 'greatest clerks' in Paris as to their meaning. He understood that they were to do with the making of the Stone, but he could not get far with his interpretation of them. At last, frustrated by twenty-one years of study and experimentation, Flamel left the country in a pilgrim's habit to seek elucidation of the book overseas.

In Leon, in Spain, he was directed to a Jewish merchant who was known to be 'very skilful in sublime sciences.' This Master Canches was overjoyed to see copies of the figures that Flamel had brought with him and implied that they were from a most important text which had been thought lost. He and Flamel returned to France together so that Canches could translate and decipher the whole of the book. Canches died before reaching Paris, but he had already given Flamel enough knowledge of the principles of alchemy for him to begin the process again in a different manner, and we are told that Nicholas and Perenelle finally made the Elixir together, which was immediately recognizable 'by the strong scent and odour thereof.' They performed the projection with the Elixir and transmuted mercury into gold, a gold 'better assuredly than common gold, more soft and pliable.' The story concludes by relating that they were able to give all the gold they made on this and later occasions to charity, to build hospitals and look after widows and orphans. Flamel certainly existed; his tombstone can still be seen, adorned with emblems of the Sun and Moon, in the museum of Cluny. How much of his story is true we do not know; but like the testimony of Helvetius, it gives us valuable insight into the nature of the alchemical quest. Emphasis is given in the narrative to the persistence and devotion of Flamel, to the need for him to work in ignorance for many years until he came, through destiny or luck, to meet the right teacher. His quest, like many others, was a mixture of personal effort and inspired guidance, needing half a lifetime to reach perfection.

ALCHEMY AS A
SPIRITUAL DISCIPLINE

The greedy cheat with impure hands may not
Attempt this Art, nor is it ever got
By the unlearned and rude: the vicious mind
To lust and softness given, it strikes stark blind,
So the sly wandering factor . . .
But the sage, pious man, who still adores
And loves his Maker, and his love implores,
Whoever joys to search the secret cause
And series of his works, their love and laws,
Let him draw near, and joining will with strength,
Study this Art in all her depth and length;
Then grave experience shall his consort be
Skilled in large nature's inmost mystery.
The knots and doubts his busy course and cares
Will oft disturb, till time the truth declares,
And stable patience, through all trials passed,
Brings the glad end and long hoped for, at last.[1]

The fundamental principle of the alchemical operation is that it should work on three levels of being at once—on body, soul, and spirit. The hermetic philosophy maintains that everything—animal, vegetable, and mineral—contains these three elements, but in an unawakened state. The Great Work is the process of breaking down the existing relationship between these factors, which is considered as an ignorant, inert, and unfruitful state requiring to be activated and brought to perfection. The alchemist sees this both in the materials he works with in his laboratory and in his own being. He aims to free the soul and spirit of matter and to reunite them with the body in a new and exalted form; he also attempts this task in his own life. Prayer, observation, and work are the tools he uses to activate his own spiritual, psychological, and physical faculties.

Although all mainstream alchemy embodies this triple approach in principle, yet different schools and adepts have often chosen to emphasize one of the levels in particular, and this engenders different qualities in the type of alchemy that results. Broadly speaking, alchemy emphasizing the perfection of the body usually dwells more on the metals and materials to be used, the laboratory processes, and the tangible results. This line of alchemy is the one most likely to give rise to chemical and physical discoveries in the world of science, although it is not completely of that world itself. Alchemy that gives the soul special consideration is likely to concern itself primarily with medicinal results and to seek for curative and healing agents—the art of the Elixir. It may use more vegetable than metallic matter in its work of preparation. Alchemy of the spirit puts the greatest efforts into the illumination of man himself, and may regard the physical and tangible results of alchemy as secondary. It lays emphasis on the role of contemplation within the alchemical work and tends to draw in religious and philosophical elements. The effects of alchemy of body and soul will be the subject of the next chapter; alchemy of the spirit will be the prime focus of this one.

Alchemy as Spiritual Development

To set the picture for a discussion of specific examples of spiritual alchemy, I shall give some indication of how the alchemical process works at a parallel level in the alchemist himself. This is intended to be an interpretation, rather than a complete definition. Readers interested in mystical and meditative traditions will no doubt be able to find parallels there corresponding to the alchemical symbols for the process of personal transformation.

The Primal Material that the alchemical seeker takes to work on at the spiritual level is himself. He is made in the image of God and contains the seeds of soul and spirit within him. These are, to some extent, imprisoned in the body; in order to release them that they may grow to perfection, he must summon up the will and intention to start the work and make the initial effort to dissolve this apparent unity. The body is not rejected as such, but it must be encouraged to loosen its hold upon the inner being so that the process of transformation can begin. This can be set in motion by embracing the alchemical discipline itself; the student decides to commit himself to a task that will demand the utmost in patience and concentration. His old way of life will be disrupted, since most of his resources— his money, time, and mental effort—will need to be channelled into the alchemical work. There is no immediate gratification in terms of quick results, and no guarantee of success at all. Although, in hermetic understanding, all first matter grows to gold in due course, and man himself evolves towards greater consciousness as part of a natural process, yet the change is usually too slow for individuals to perceive and experience: alchemy seeks to accelerate this change and bring about the possibility of completion within a personal life span. Thus taking on alchemical work indicates a deliberate submission to both difficulty and danger: even on the external level, as we have seen, alchemists could lose their health, their money, and even their lives in the quest.

The alchemical process, both at the laboratory and at the spiritual level, is considered irreversible, which is why the alchemist is counselled to be courageous and wholehearted about his endeavour, for he takes a true risk and has no certainty that he will ever succeed.

The labours of the alchemical work will continue to activate the faculties of the seeker, and the frustrations experienced in trying to find the right materials and correct sequence of operation will keep him alert and observant. The alchemists relate that when the initial dissolution has taken place, the Mercurial water can be extracted and reserved for future use. This 'water' corresponds to the elements of hope and faith the aspirant discovers within himself. All men and women have some intimation or experience of the divine in their lives, but sometimes this is locked away or rendered impotent by doubt. The first stage of dissolution allows a person to see this 'treasure' for what it really is. It should then be 'stored away' safely ready for later use, rather than subjected to the upheavals and even violence of the subsequent stages. Then, when there is resolution of the conflict (corresponding to the stage where the 'child' is born in the vessel), it can be added or released to nurture the growing creation with hope and love.

After the alchemical material has been prepared and put through the initial stages of dissolution and activation, it is heated in the sealed vessel. The sealed vessel corresponds to the secrecy with which the work is carried out, an important ingredient of spiritual discipline. The aspirant must be willing to keep his own counsel, confiding only in his teacher, if he has one—otherwise all is lost through evaporation or dissipation. (This is similar to the creative process in the arts, where the writer, musician, or painter does not subject the work in progress to outside opinion or advice until it is fully 'born,' to prevent the inspiration and energy from disappearing completely.)

What is the heat that is applied to the vessel? One interpretation is that the student keeps his aim always to the fore, like a fire burning within him. This corresponds to the 'burning love' of the mystics, without which they would lose heart and lack the courage to face the difficulties they encounter. Another aspect is that the student may be asked by his teacher to perform demanding tasks in the laboratory that stretch him to his limits of endurance. Friction, as we all know, produces heat! Even if the flames spring up from anger, indignation, and outrage they can still be a very effective force. However, in alchemy it is stated that the heat must be carefully regulated, otherwise the vessel may be cracked and broken: the energies the alchemist expends on laboratory work, research, and religious prayer must all be tempered or else a harmful frenzy or mania can result.

In the apparatus, the liquid is circulated over and over again, being distilled and redistilled to a degree that most scientists would consider pointless. The alchemists maintain that this is the only way to further the transformation of the material. If the action is performed with patience, attention, and care, it will have results on the psychological level too. It is similar to certain religious and meditational practices, such as the orthodox Christian discipline of the 'prayer of the heart,' which consists of repeating silently a short and simple prayer over and over again until it becomes a ceaseless and perpetual activity. Such repetitive practices are far from meaningless if carried out correctly and can lead to an experience of deeper and more significant levels of consciousness, releasing potent and vital energies that will help to fuel the transformation.

This concept is made explicit in a Chinese text, *The Secret of the Golden Flower,* which comes from an alchemical-mystical tradition. The book itself may date from around the eighth or ninth century AD, although it was passed down orally until its first printing in the eighteenth century. The work contains instruction for meditation, a method based on the discipline of 'circulation of the light.' The light is within a person and the meditation causes it to circulate and crystallize into the Elixir: the moment of crystallization is likened to the union of male and female and the birth of a 'seed pearl.'

> The Golden Flower is the light. What colour is the light? One uses the Golden Flower as a symbol. It is the true energy of the transcendent great One . . . When the light circulates, the energies of the whole body appear before its throne, as, when a holy king has established the capital and has laid down the fundamental rules of order, all the

states approach with tribute . . . Therefore you have only to make the light circulate: that is the deepest and most wonderful secret. The light is easy to move, but difficult to fix. If it is made to circulate long enough, then it crystallizes itself; that is the natural spirit body . . . The Golden Flower is the Elixir of Life. All changes of spiritual consciousness depend upon the heart. There is a secret charm which, although it works very accurately, is yet so fluid that it needs extreme intelligence and clarity, and the most complete absorption and tranquillity . . . The way to the Elixir of Life is known as supreme magic, seed-water, spirit-fire, and thought-earth: these three. What is seed-water? It is the true, one energy of former heaven. Spirit-fire is the light. Thought-earth is the heavenly heart of the middle dwelling [intuition] . . . [By circulating the light] one returns to the Creative. If this method is followed, plenty of seed-water will be present of itself; the spirit-fire will be ignited, and the thought-earth will solidify and crystallize. And thus the holy fruit matures.[2]

From its earliest recorded history, alchemy has contained all the ingredients necessary for a discipline that is to be practised within one's own being as well as in the laboratory retort. The process is described in terms of living beings—of dragons, fishes, birds, and of human archetypes, such as the king and queen, images which speak to us of our own nature. We remember the vision of Zosimos, where he meets the priest who has 'undergone intolerable violence' and concludes that the aspiring alchemist must build a temple, seek the opening, and perform the sacrifice himself. The identification of the alchemist with his work is the chief distinction between alchemy and science, for while the scientist stands outside the experiment as far as possible in order to obtain 'objective' results, the alchemist only values results that are obtained by personal effort and involvement.

So the symbolism of alchemy, with its mythical battles, deaths, and resurrections of living beings, can be discerned as readily in the processes of one's own psyche as in the sealed vessel. Even the four elements of earth, water, fire, and air must be brought into the correct balance in the personal realm; special attention is paid to the mastery of fire and water, for these two elements are contrary to one another in their action and are mutually destructive. The reconciliation of fire and water was a central aim in the process of perfection: 'The things that are in the realms above are also in the realms beneath; what heaven shows is often found on earth. Fire and flowing water are contrary to one another; Happy thou, if thou canst unite them: let it suffice thee to know this!'[3]

This process was often symbolized by the seal of Solomon, the double triangle interlaced with one apex pointing upwards and one down, representing the uniting of the heavenly and earthly principles. In *The Golden Age Restored*, Henry Madathanas reports a mystical experience in which Solomon himself showed him the secrets of the seal and opened his understanding. The elements were seen as existing on more than one level, having far greater significance than a mere physical lump of earth or pool of water. The author of the *Sophic Hydrolith* says that the 'Fire of the Sages,' a chief agent of the alchemical process, lies hidden in 'our substance' and that it must be roused and fanned into a flame before it can be effective. Water will become the regenerating principle, when we have passed through the furnace of affliction ourselves and the spiritual death is accomplished. In this case the connection between alchemy and spiritual growth is explicit; in other cases the symbols used are capable of interpretation at both laboratory and personal level.

The 'spiritual alchemists' frequently made much use of the doctrine of the three principles—Mercury, Salt, and Sulphur. The terms were presumably chosen because the physical substances of mercury, salt, and sulphur embodied some of the qualities of the three forces as they were understood, but it should be realized that the significance of alchemical Mercury, Salt, and Sulphur was not restricted to this level. Basilius Valentinus, one of the most famous of alchemists (probably *fl.* sixteenth century), described the formative process in this way—and this extract shows just how complex some of the concepts could be:

> Know that our seed is produced in the following way. A celestial influence descends from above, by the decree and ordinance of God, and mingles with the astral properties. When this union has taken place, the two bring forth a third, namely, an earth-like substance, which is the principle of our seed, of its first source, so that it can shew an ancestry, and from which three the elements, such as water, air, and earth, take their origin. These elements work underground in the form of fire, and there produce what Hermes, and all who have preceded me, call the three first principles, viz., the internal soul, the impalpable spirit, and visible bodies, beyond which we can find no earlier beginning of our Magistery.

> In the course of time these three unite, and are changed through the action of fire into a palpable substance, viz., quicksilver, sulphur and salt. If these three substances be mixed, they are hardened and coagulated into a perfect body, which represents the

> seed chosen and appointed by the Creator . . . If you can only
> rectify the Mercury, Sulphur, and Salt . . . until the metallic spirit
> and body are inseparably joined together by means of the metal-
> lic soul, you thereby firmly rivet the chain of love, and prepare the
> palace for the coronation.[4]

The three principles could therefore be understood as operating throughout the universe, in the most sublime realms as well as in the world of
Nature. The sulphur of Nature, for instance, said Michael Sendivogius, is
the influence that produces smells and colours and imparts understanding to animals. Sulphur is imprisoned and must be set free by alchemy; its
release in the alchemical vessel is in no way different from the release of
Sulphur—or spirit—in ourselves, for:

> When he [Sulphur] is set free, he binds his gaolers, and gives their
> three kingdoms to his deliverer. He also gives to him a magic mir-
> ror, in which the three parts of the wisdom of the whole world may
> be seen and known at a glance: and this mirror clearly exhibits the
> creation of the world, the influences of the celestial virtues of earthly
> things, and the way in which Nature composed substances by the
> regulation of heat.[5]

In most alchemical texts it becomes obvious that Mercury, as the soul, is
the chief agent in alchemy, mediating between body and spirit and performing the transformations at each stage. Salt, the body, must perish and
be resurrected, and Sulphur, the spirit, must soar like the eagle and attain
to knowledge. The texts show over and over again that knowledge and
wisdom were devoutly sought by the alchemists: Sendivogius calls the
alchemists 'the children of knowledge.' The aspirations of the alchemists
are clearly shown; sometimes the Great Work is illustrated in pictorial
form as a mountain up which the seeker must climb, encountering dangers and trials at every turn of the path. Sometimes, especially in the earlier Graeco-Roman texts, the insights of alchemy come as part of a great
revelation of the universal scheme of things, as when Ostanes is guided
through the seven gates of existence to learn the secrets of natural and
celestial influences. Sometimes these gates, or mountains, will be closely
associated with the planets, which were seen as corresponding with hier-
archical levels of existence (from the moon, the closest, to Saturn, the
most distant) and with the metals that were associated with these planets.
Again, the physical properties of the planets are not the most important

aspect of this sequence, for the planets were thought to relate to a whole realm of being, governing aspects of man's psyche and spirit, and corresponding also to angelic kingdoms. The alchemist was often exhorted to search for the Primal Matter on the summit of a mountain:

> On the other side of the fourth leaf, he painted a fair flower on the top of a very high mountain, which was sore shaken with the north wind: it had the foot blue, the flowers white and red, the leaves shining like fine gold, and round about it the dragons and griffons of the North made their nests and abode . . . [6]

The words from Figure XL of *The Book of Lambspring* show poignantly how the alchemist must aspire to the heights and then return to the earth to carry out the Great Work:

> Here is an old father of Israel,
> Who has an only Son,
> A Son whom he loves with all his heart.
> With sorrow he prescribes sorrow to him.
> He commits him to a guide,
> Who is to conduct him whithersoever he will.
> The Guide addresses the Son in these words:
> Come hither! I will conduct thee everywhere,
> To the summit of the loftiest mountain,
> That thou mayest understand all wisdom,
> That thou mayest behold the greatness of the earth, and of the sea
> And thence derive true pleasure. I will bear thee through the air
> To the gates of the highest heaven.
> The Son hearkened to the words of the Guide,
> And ascended upward with him;
> There saw he the heavenly throne,
> That was beyond measure glorious.
> When he had beheld these things,
> He remembered his Father with sighing,
> Pitied the great sorrow of his Father,
> And said: I will return to his breast.

It can be readily seen that the main body of alchemical literature contains symbolism potent enough to relate to human spiritual transformation, and that it is frequently explicit in its exhortations to the seeker to search for perfection and wisdom in his own being, as well as in his laboratory experiments.

Alchemy and Christianity

In Europe, the tradition of spiritual alchemy became strongly identified with Christianity, and the alchemical operation was explained as the mystical path through which the individual could become one with Christ, who is himself the perfect Stone.

The earliest source that draws the parallel between alchemy and Christianity is identified by C. G. Jung as the *Margarita Pretiosa,* written by Petrus Bonus of Ferrar in the fourteenth century. By the sixteenth and seventeenth centuries this approach had become well established, and authors exercised their metaphysical ingenuity in drawing correspondences between Christian and alchemical teaching.

In *The Sophic Hydrolith,* the life of Jesus is equated with the transformation of the Stone in the alchemical process. The fire that heats the material is like the 'furnace of affliction' that Jesus had to pass through when he was rejected and insulted by men.

The period of 'chemical digestion,' the forty-day gestation period of the seed in the vessel, is like the forty-day-and-night fast that Christ spent in the wilderness. And the life of Christ has given us the elements we need for personal redemption, for his baptism and crucifixion are the water and spirit that will regenerate us when we have ourselves passed through the furnace and come to the 'true black Raven's head,' the mortification when beauty and reputation are lost and intense suffering is experienced. This particular text shows that alchemy can be a truly spiritual and Christian discipline, whilst retaining a concern with practical alchemy; other writers, however, began to pay less attention to the laboratory aspects of the work and teach alchemy purely as a devotional and mystical discipline.

The most famous of these is **Jacob Boehme** (1575–1624), whose writings are highly complex and enigmatic, containing descriptions of man's relationships to God and Christ couched in alchemical terms. Boehme's knowledge of alchemy was profound, and he used the principles of the alchemical process to explain how man might evolve from an unawakened and undeveloped state into a fully conscious being. Boehme began life as an untutored shoemaker having little concern for religious matters. The story of his conversion is related as follows:

> One day while tending his master's shoe shop, a mysterious stranger entered who, while he seemed to possess but little of this world's goods, appeared to be most wise and noble in spiritual attainment. The stranger asked the price of a pair of shoes, but young Boehme did not dare to name a figure, for fear that he would displease his master. The stranger insisted and Boehme finally placed a valuation which he felt was all that his master possibly could hope to secure for the shoes. The stranger immediately bought them and departed. A short distance down the street the mysterious stranger stopped and cried out in a loud voice, 'Jakob, Jakob, come forth.' In amazement and fright, Boehme ran out of the house. The strange man fixed his eyes upon the youth—great eyes which sparkled and seemed filled with divine light. He took the boy's right hand and addressed him as follows: 'Jakob, thou art little, but shalt be great, and become another man, such a one as at whom the world shall wonder.[7]

Boehme saw that the conflict induced between the warring elements in the alchemical vessel was an emblem of the activity of nature itself. Without conflict there could be no movement, no difference between created beings, and no motivation to bring about change and improvement:

> For the eternal nature has produced nothing in its desire, except a likeness out of itself; and if there were not an everlasting mixing, there would be an eternal peace in nature, but so nature would not be revealed and made manifest, in the combat it becomes manifest; so that each thing elevates itself, and would get out of the combat into the still rest, and so it runs to and fro, and thereby only awakens and stirs up the combat.

This essential combat is to be cured finally by 'the light of nature' and by 'the desire of the spirit.' Boehme's summary of the alchemical spiritual work is as follows:

> [Man] lies now shut up after his fall in a gross, deformed, bestial dead image; he is not like an angel, much less like unto paradise; he is as the gross ore in Saturn, wherein the gold is couched and shut up; his paradisical image is in him as if it were not, and it is also not manifest, the outward body is a stinking carcass, while it yet lives in the poison; he is a bad thorny bush, from whence notwithstanding

fair rose-buds may bloom forth, and grow out of the thorns, and manifest that which lies hidden, and shut up in the wrathful poison-ful Mercury, till the artist who has made him takes him in hand, and brings the living Mercury into his gold or paradisical image disap-peared and shut up in death; so that the inclosed image, which was created out of the divine meekness and love-essentiality, may again bud and spring forth in the divine Mercury, viz. in the word of the Deity, which entered in the humanity shut up . . .

And then the divine Mercury changes the wrathful Mercury into its property, and Christ is born, who bruises the head of the serpent . . . and a new a man arises in holiness and righteousness, which . . . appears and puts forth its lustre as the hidden gold out of the earthly property.[8]

Every now and then there is a fusion between two traditions of knowl-edge; when this happens a new mode of inspiration arises. Boehme's injection of alchemy into Christianity inspired many of the mystics and thinkers who succeeded him. Even though the alchemical allusions them-selves finally dwindled away in the Christian context, yet alchemy had proved itself a potent force. Two other writers of the seventeenth century famous for their interest in alchemy and their descriptions of it in terms of Christian mysticism are Henry and Thomas Vaughan. The Vaughans were twins, born in Breconshire in 1621, and both studied at Oxford. Thomas, the lesser known of the two, had a colourful career as a doctor, as a priest finally expelled from his living, and as an alchemist. Henry (1621-95), now known as a fine mystical poet, read Law and held the sedate post of secretary to Judge Lloyd. Thomas (1621-66), interested in spiritual mat-ters and a keeper of a vivid dream diary, experimented and worked at alchemy under the patronage of another famous 'chymist' of the day, Sir Robert Murrey, Secretary of State for Scotland. He wrote frequently under the pseudonym of 'Eugenius Philalethes'; his style is stirring, though he lacks the polish of his more poetical brother. His exhortations are to fol-low the path of Christianity as revealed through the alchemical teachings:

Truth calls to man: 'Be ye transmuted . . . be ye transmuted from dead stones into living philosophical stones. I am the true Medicine, rectifying and transmuting that which is no more into that which it was before corruption, and into something better by far, and that which is not into that which it ought to be. Lo, I am at the door of your conscience, knocking night and day, and ye will not open unto me, yet I stand mildly waiting . . . Come again and again, often come, ye who seek wisdom . . . O sonorous voice, O voice sweet and gracious to the ears of the sages, O fount of inexhaustible riches to those thirsting after truth and justice! O solace to the need of those who are desolate! Why seek ye further, anxious mortals?'[9]

Henry Vaughan, the poet, certainly understood the hermetic practice, but it is not known to what extent he carried out alchemical experiments. In his poetry he drew upon the mystical aspects of alchemy: poems such as 'The Night,' 'Cock-crowing,' or 'A Vision of Time and Eternity' provide convincing evidence that Vaughan was using alchemy not simply as a literary device, but that he had a deep understanding of its inner meaning and used this to fire his creative work:

> Father of lights! what sunny seed,
> What glance of day hast thou confined
> Into this bird? To all the breed
> This busy ray thou hast assigned;
>> Their magnetism works all night,
>> And dreams of Paradise and light.
>
> Their eyes watch for the morning hue,
> Their little grain expelling night
> So shines and sings, as if it knew
> The path unto the house of light,
>> It seems their candle, howe'r done,
>> Was tinned and lighted at the sun.
>
> If such a tincture, such a touch,
> So firm a longing can impower
> Shall thy own image think it much
> To watch for thy appearing hour?
>> If a mere blast so fill the sail,
>> Shall not the breath of God prevail?[10]

Alchemy and Philosophy

From the late fifteenth century onwards, a general movement arose in European circles of learning and nobility that attempted to draw together all the strands of artistic, scientific, and occult disciplines, and to weave them into one universal system of knowledge. Subjects such as alchemy and astrology, whose philosophy encompassed the mundane, the human, and the divine worlds, became the central focus of this new worldview. Because of this, they lost some of their individual identity as traditions in their own right, but at the same time they released their inherent creative energy into a broader field of study.

One major stimulus to the formation of a universal philosophy was the rediscovery of the Hermetic texts in 1460. Cosimo de' Medici of Italy was at that time employing agents to scour the world for manuscripts that might bring to light lost classics from the ancient Greek and Egyptian worlds. A monk presented him with a manuscript that proved to be a collection of many of the 'lost' texts ascribed to **Hermes Trismegistus**, a collection now known as the *Corpus Hermeticum*. Hermes, closely associated with the Egyptian god Thoth, was said to have been a great Egyptian priest who had lived centuries before Christ. The writings under his name were widely revered, for here, it was thought, were the genuine and original teachings of Egypt, giving the true revelation of how the world was created, of how the cosmos was structured, of the powers of man, and of the meaning of all occult and astrological practices. It derived, so its readers thought, from 'a pure golden age of magic';[11] it apparently affirmed the truth of Christianity by referring to the existence of the divine Son; and it showed that the occult arts could be part of religious belief rather than demonic practices. The Hermetic texts did not perhaps introduce much that was new into the world of alchemy and allied subjects, but they appeared to lend authority and reason to them and to give them the unquestionable stamp of ancient approval. It should be remembered that at this time anyone wishing to prove a point of principle had only to show that some former sage had said the very same thing: any argument could be clinched by an appropriate reference to the ancient classical masters. What better, for alchemy, than to show that Hermes Trismegistus himself had underwritten its validity?

Unfortunately, it was later discovered by Isaac Casaubon in 1614 that the texts did not pre-date Christ. We now know them to be the products of the first two or three centuries AD, composed by Greeks and containing strong Gnostic, Jewish, and Neoplatonic influences. They may well contain elements of far earlier teachings, but they do not enshrine the wisdom of ancient Egypt. Nevertheless, even after 1614, they continued to exert a considerable fascination for alchemists and occult philosophers, the subtleties of observation and grandeur of cosmology contained in certain of the books being valued on their own account, whenever they originated. They affirmed the principle of alchemy that Nature was the divine force of change operating within the Universe:

> The Kosmos also . . . has sense and thought; but its sense and thought are of a kind peculiar to itself, not like the sense and thought of man, nor varying like his, but mightier and less diversified. The sense and thought of the Kosmos are occupied solely in making all things, and dissolving them again into itself. The Kosmos is an instrument of God's will; and it was made by him to this end, that, having received from God the seeds of all things that belong to it, and keeping these seeds within itself, it might bring all things into actual existence. The Kosmos produces life in all things by its movement; and decomposing them, it renews the things that have been decomposed; for, like a good husbandman, it gives them renewal by sowing seed . . . And rightly is the Kosmos so named, for all things in it are wrought into an ordered whole by the diversity of births and the incessant continuance of life, and by its unwearied activity, and the swiftness of its movement, and the immutable necessity that rules in it, and by the combining of the elements, and the fit disposal of all things that come into being.[12]

Man, the Hermetic texts say, was created a being like God himself, made of Life and Light. He came to know the 'administrators,' the planets that rule over destiny, and 'received a share of their nature.' But through will, he penetrated further into the created levels of the world, further into the realms of matter, until he was revealed to Nature. Nature fell in love with man and enticed him to live on her earth.

> And that is why man, unlike all other living creatures upon earth, is twofold. He is mortal by reason of his body; he is immortal by reason of the Man of eternal substance. He is immortal, and has all things in his power; yet he suffers the lot of a mortal, being subject to Destiny. He is exalted above the structure of the heavens; yet he is born a slave of Destiny.[13]

The task of Man is to have the courage and will to develop his powers and attain to knowledge:

> If then you do not make yourself equal to God, you cannot appre-
> hend God; for like is known by like. Leap clear of all that is corporeal,
> and make yourself grow to a like expanse with that greatness which
> is beyond all measure; rise above all time and become eternal; then
> you will apprehend God. Think that for you too nothing is impossi-
> ble; deem that you too are immortal, and that you are able to grasp
> all things in your thought, to know every craft and science; find your
> home in the haunts of every living creature; make yourself higher
> than all heights and lower than all depths, bring together in yourself
> all opposites of quality, heat and cold, dryness and fluidity; think that
> you are everywhere at once, on land, at sea, in heaven; think that
> you are not yet begotten, that you are in the womb, that you are
> young, that you are old, that you have died, that you are in the world
> beyond the grave; grasp in your thought all this at once, all times and
> places, all substances and qualities and magnitudes together; then
> you can apprehend God. But if you shut up your soul in your body,
> and abase yourself, and say 'I know nothing, I can do nothing; I am
> afraid of earth and sea, I cannot mount to heaven; I know not what
> I was, nor what I shall be,' then what have you to do with God? [14]

On this basis, there was nothing to be ashamed of in alchemy, for what was it but a search for God through his manifestations in Nature, carried out with the power of thought and skill of craft that God had bestowed on man so that he might understand better the secrets of the creation? In another respect, it did away with the old emphasis on choosing alchemy itself as a pathway, as a mistress the alchemist served with unceasing devo-tion. Men of learning chose more and more to combine occult arts and rational sciences in their quest for an ever wider worldview. They were not content to be bound by the obscure world of the laboratory and the daily attention to lengthy alchemical operations. It becomes hard to trace, in alchemical writers of this period, whether their alchemy was of a purely spiritual, intellectual, or practical type, or whether it was a combination of these approaches.

The opening up of alchemy, and its incorporation into new philoso-phies and schools of learning, meant that it provided a powerful leavening for the seekers of the period but became less and less distinguishable as a practice in its own right. For instance, it was a vital ingredient of Rosi-crucianism. This esoteric movement is the subject of much controversy.

It first came to prominence in 1614–15, when two texts—the *Fama Fraternitatis* and the *Confessio Fraternitatis*—appeared that told a strange tale of a secret society and a brotherhood that was ready to meet the dawning of a new age: 'Now there remains yet that which in short time . . . shall be spoke and uttered forth, when the World shall awake out of her heavy and drowsy sleep, and with an open heart, bare-head, and bare-foot, shall merrily and joyfully meet the new arising Sun.' The tale in the *Fama* is that of one Brother Rosenkreuz (RC), who, a century or two before, had travelled widely in search of wisdom and learning and had founded an Order whose members were to devote themselves to this end. The members, first four and then seven in number, were bound by obligation to use their skills to cure the sick and to take no money for their services. They were to wear whatever dress was customary for the country that they were in and were requested to meet together once a year.

The anonymous writer declared that the Order was still in existence, fortified by the recent discovery of the tomb of RC, which is described in precise and complex detail, indicating that it was laid out more as an occult temple than a grave. He implied that the Brethren were now seeking those of like mind to join them in preparation for the advent of wisdom into the world. The wisdom as formulated by the Order was to be of universal relevance, a synthesis of the best and most profound philosophy known to man. It would be 'a compendium of the Universe,' the 'perfection [of] all Arts,' 'so that finally man might thereby understand his own nobleness and worth, and why he is called Microcosmus, and how far his knowledge extendeth into Nature.'

The response was overwhelming. People wrote and published letters begging to be taken into the Order, while others condemned the heresy and presumption of the Brethren. No one openly admitted to being a member of the Order, but yet there soon grew up a body of literature and art that we can now classify as 'Rosicrucian.' It developed its own themes and identity, tying together Qabalism, Christianity, alchemy, and astrology, as well as music, mathematics, geometry, and architecture. As time went on, the reality of Rosicrucian brotherhoods was more readily admitted (one of the most intriguing by name being an American branch entitled The Woman in the Wilderness, devoted chiefly to the practice of spiritual alchemy), but by the mid-eighteenth century the early freshness and vitality had gone out of the concepts and emblems.

Some scholars maintain that the Order never really existed in the seventeenth century, since Johann Valentin Andreae, from Tübingen, is said to have confessed to writing *The Chymical Wedding of Christian Rosenkreuz* as a joke. Dame Frances Yates, on the other hand, in *The Rosicrucian Enlightenment,* believed that the predominant motive of the proclamations was political, and that the ill-fated Frederic, Emperor of Bohemia, was the agent of a plan to set up a utopian Rosicrucian state in which the universal philosophy would be the guiding light of its subjects' lives. It is perhaps more likely that the Order emerged publicly from a pre-existing occult group or brotherhood, which may have used a different name and which judged the time was ripe to generate public interest but deliberately created myth and mystery around its supposed origins and existence.

The works of writers such as Michael Maier, Heinrich Khunrath, and Robert Fludd typify Rosicrucian literature and show how large a part alchemy played in it. According to one authority, Heinrich Khunrath, although he died in 1605, before the official 'launch' of Rosicrucianism, 'bears within the compass of his books all the elements that we recognize later in the Rosicrucian publications.'[15] He was in contact with, among others, John Dee and Emperor Rudolf of Prague, both of whom are thought to form links in the Rosicrucian chain. His Amphitheatre of Eternal Wisdom, with its very fine engravings, is a good example of how Rosicrucian illustrations differed from those of traditional alchemy. The latter usually set out to illustrate each stage of the alchemical process in turn, using mythical symbols often shown in dramatic interaction with each other (two lions fighting, etc.). The Rosicrucian tendency is to give a complete picture of the quest in each illustration, including as many different aspects of it as possible in order to denote completeness of vision. For instance, in the engravings 'The Journey to the Heights' and 'The Castle of the Mysteries,' the whole search is shown from start to finish, with men setting out, working, traveling by boat, meeting with others, contemplating, praying, and so on. The landscapes are complex, and symmetry, proportion, and perspective are used to make symbolic points. There are inscriptions on various parts of the drawing, and the flavour is that of a vision explained in structured terms. Khunrath did not neglect alchemy proper. A laboratory is shown in detail in 'The First Stage of the Great Work,' but the room is also equipped with an oratory (in which the aspirant is shown praying) as well as musical and mathematical equipment. Alchemy was thus no longer seen as an exclusive art; it was brought into line with other disciplines in order to create a harmonious philosophy.

The Rosicrucian manifestos mention alchemy by name, and they curse the blindness of those who seek gold as a goal in its own right. It is the province of 'many runagates and roguish people [who] use great villainies and cozen and abuse the credit which is given them.' Those who want merely to transmute metals are not true philosophers. But Brother RC himself understood the art:

> Whatsoever has been said in the *Fama* concerning the deceivers against the transmutation of metals, and the highest medicine in the world, the same is thus to be understood, that this is so great gift of God we do in no manner set at naught, or despise it. But because she bringeth not with her always the knowledge of Nature, but this bringeth forth not only medicine, but also maketh manifest and open unto us innumerable secrets and wonders. Therefore it is requisite, that we be earnest to attain to the understanding and knowledge of philosophy. And moreover, excellent wits ought not to be drawn to the tincture of metals, before they be exercised well in the knowledge of Nature.[16]

We have little evidence of how the Rosicrucians applied their philosophy and learning in terms of individual development. The only clues come from writers who seem to bear the Rosicrucian identity, even if they do not admit to being one of the brotherhood. Such a one is **Robert Fludd** (1574–1637). He was the son of Sir Thomas Fludd, a military administrator, and was educated at Oxford. In 1598 he spent six years traveling as a tutor on the Continent, during which time he probably developed his medical and occult interests, partly through contact with Paracelsians (see Chapter 7). He returned to England and took his degree in medicine, setting up practice in London, and was renowned for his successful personal effect upon his patients. But he came into conflict with the medical authorities because of his unorthodox views and his bluntness in expressing them. Fludd was celibate and devoted himself entirely to his medical practice and to his exploration of philosophy through his knowledge of music, alchemy, and science. His greatest work is the *History of the Macrocosm and the Microcosm,* in which he attempts to describe the divine and the human worlds and the way in which they interact.

Fludd did not openly admit to membership of the Rosicrucian Order, but he wrote an essay in its defence that expounded its virtues and the necessity of accomplishing the 'mystical building' of the rose and the cross for oneself:

> The Alchemist transmutes the apparent forms into occult ones by finding the general form through destruction of the specific one. This is the work of the true and divine Alchemy, through the mediation of which the earthly has been opened to the entry of the joys of Paradise so that men may pluck that red rose with the lilies of the field and taste of the Tree of Life.

A spiritual, and Christian, form of alchemy seems to have been a central theme for Fludd, and it may be that he distinguished this from 'laboratory' alchemy, which, in his diagrams, he lists equally with other arts and sciences, describing it only as 'art correcting Nature in the mineral realm.' One has the impression that his interest would not be held for long by mere metals and minerals. Additionally, there is a hint that he is keen to put Nature in her proper place. Nature was equated with beauty, truth, and wisdom by some alchemists, who made her their inspiration in the hermetic work; but to Fludd, she was 'not a goddess, but the proximate minister of God, at whose behest she governs the sub-celestial worlds.'

All in all, it seems that Fludd was more concerned to perceive the processes of creation through his intellect and imagination than in the alchemical retort. His emblems are of the creation of the world, of the elements, of the stature of man. Yet, in the specific context of his medical practice, he did make use of alchemical knowledge. It was an inherent part of the Rosicrucian philosophy that if all disciplines could be traced to one set of principles, then, likewise, one discipline could combine with or shed light on another, for particularly effective results. It is recorded that Fludd made use of 'magnetism' in his healing, and that he created a salve to heal wounds that was placed not on the wound but on the weapon that had caused the wound (this aroused not a little controversy). Even closer to the alchemical philosophy were his attempts to explain certain medical conditions:

> The origin of Catarrh—Here we see water converted by the fire's heat into a vapour, which ascends from the pot and meets the lid, whose lower temperature makes it condense into drops. It is even so with the human body: the watery phlegm originates in the southerly region of the intestines, and in disease is heated by the fire of the liver; it rises to the colder region of the head, where again it coalesces in warm droplets. These are the cause of colds, catarrh and coryza, and from this phlegm in the head one suffers their side-effects of headaches, impaired hearing and vertigo.[17]

Alchemy thus expanded from a closely knit discipline into a tool for scientific and biological understanding, as well as into a spiritual teaching that was no longer dependent upon work carried out in a laboratory, and from the seventeenth century the history of 'pure' alchemy becomes harder to follow as it merges with other philosophies and traditions.

APPLIED ALCHEMY

Alchemy has borne fruit in the realms of medicine, science, and literature. Many of those who have been inspired by its philosophy and imagery were themselves practising alchemists, but often their alchemical skills have been overshadowed by their successes in the more conventional areas of the sciences and arts. The view is frequently taken by contemporary writers that the sole function of alchemy was to provide a starting point for the more 'objective' sciences and that by the eighteenth century, when the new era of physics, chemistry, and medicine was firmly established, alchemy had become redundant. The more esoteric aspects of alchemy are often regarded as the necessary, but rather regrettable, means by which alchemy grew until it could be turned into a proper science. A twentieth-century chemist will naturally be interested in alchemy mainly as it relates to the history of laboratory equipment and experiment, but to exclude all other considerations is to take too narrow a view; for since alchemy has been a source of inspiration for physicists, doctors, mystics, writers, and psychologists, its power as a way of knowledge in its own right must be recognized. Alchemy rests on principles that have a deep relevance to man's work and progress in the world. The principles may be clothed in forms which are archaic or even erroneous in their assumptions, but these do not invalidate the principles themselves, as is often glibly assumed. Alchemy is like a central spindle, from which threads are unwound and taken into other contexts, eventually severing their original connection; but the spindle remains and can be used again after years of neglect.

Paracelsus and Alchemical Medicine

Theophrastus Bombastus von Hohenheim, better known as Paracelsus (1493–1541), was born near Zurich. His father was a physican, and after his mother died they moved together to Villach (now in Austria), where Paracelsus grew up. The whole course of his life was marked by an avid curiosity to learn at first hand, to investigate and experiment on his own account, without being tied to traditional doctrines. He observed, questioned, argued, and practised. The first known phase of his study began when he joined Sigismund Fugger, who owned mines and metal workshops in the Tyrol; here he learnt about the principles of mining and the ways in which minerals and metals could be used. Fugger himself was an alchemist, so alchemy was probably a very early topic of study for Paracelsus.

Training in occult matters may have come from a contact with **Johannes Trithemius** (1462–1516), who was abbot of the monastery at Sponheim. In his youth, before he became a monk, Trithemius was said to have received instruction in secret sciences from a mysterious teacher, who then told him that on his journey home to Trittenheim he would find the key to his life. As he travelled, he was forced to shelter from the snow at the Benedictine Monastery of Sponheim and decided never to leave it. He entered the Order, becoming abbot after only a year. He restored discipline and order amongst the monks, who had become lazy, and built up a magnificent library covering all the branches of learning. His own learning embraced the Qabalah and the neoplatonic doctrines of universal harmony that preceded Rosicrucianism. As might be expected, he was at times accused of practising black magic, but he defended his position with the words: 'I am a lover of Divine Wisdom—in man and in Nature. This is the Magic I follow.' His pupils are thought to have included **Cornelius Agrippa**, and his writings such as the *Steganographia,* which dealt with the relationship between man, astrology, and the angels, were eagerly sought after by men such as John Dee.

We can infer from influences such as those of Fugger and Trithemius that Paracelsus was determined to expand his sphere of knowledge and bring the very highest and best into the medicine he practised. He also had a great respect for the native wisdom of peasants and gypsies, whom he saw as true observers of Nature as opposed to hypocritical scholars whom he condemned. He had no respect for authority as such, was frequently drunk and badly dressed, always ready to quarrel, and, as might be gathered, made himself many enemies. He travelled widely throughout Europe, possibly in the East as well, and he claimed to have taken the last boat out from Rhodes before the Turks invaded, which might link him with the Knights of St. John (see p. 70). His professional status came to its peak when he was offered the post of City Physician and Professor of Medicine at Basel University after he had cured Johann Froben, a well-to-do printer who had been suffering from a serious and perplexing illness.

But Paracelsus soon made himself unpopular by refusing to worship at the shrine of Galen, Avicenna, and Aristotle, whose writings were accorded the authority of Scripture by the medical practitioners of the day. He even burnt some of the sacred volumes in public and insulted the unquestioning physicians of his time in almost everything he wrote, calling them 'sausage-stuffers,' 'clownish concocters,' 'imposters,' and 'ignorant sprouts'! After an unhappy lawsuit, Paracelsus hurriedly left Basel and spent most of his remaining years traveling in Germany and Austria. Although many of his words had fallen on deaf ears, yet there were some students who listened and took note. After his death in 1541, his followers grew in number until by about 1570 a definite Paracelsian school existed, and his influence spread until he is now considered as a key figure in the birth not only of modern orthodox medicine but also of homeopathic medicine, whose principles accord closely with his teachings.

His writings are numerous and complex, and it is not clear which are original works and which were composed by his pupils. Today there is a tendency to label his interests separately—as alchemy, astrology, pharmacy, magic, etc.; but to Paracelsus they were all one, and indeed he considered that they should interact if medicine was to be effective. It is impossible to summarize all his ideas here, but a sketch of those that are particularly relevant to alchemy follows.

Paracelsus *was* an alchemist and he gives a remarkably lucid exposition of the process in *The Archidoxes of Magic*. The starting point, he explains, is to mix the 'Philosopher's Mercury' with common mercury, these being the male and female, fixed and volatile principles, which will destroy each other before becoming fixed in a new union. The seed is produced and the 'pregnancy' may be diagnosed by the 'blackening' of the matter. Good auguries of growth are shown by the 'various flowers of divers colours' (the Peacock's Tail), and in due course the matter becomes white, forming the Lunar Stone, then yellow, and finally red, which is the perfect or Solar Stone.

A key feature of Paracelsian alchemy and medicine was the importance of celestial energies and influences. Planets and metals were associated; gold, for instance, was influenced by the sun as it grew to perfection in the earth and was itself an emblem of solar power. Each metal was related to a specific planet and was said to contain within itself an 'arcanum,' a celestial power derived directly from its ruling planet. This arcanum could be released and perfected through the alchemical process and then used as an effective medicine. Modern chemists view this as the first real attempt to select out the active ingredient in a substance through chemical processes.

Carrying out such alchemical work, Paracelsus maintained, was like recreating the Universe in miniature. Conditions in the vessel must be engendered so that the precise arcanum would manifest itself, just as the corresponding planet had come to birth in the original creation of the world. He said that the alchemical furnace should be made like the firmament itself, 'fit and apt for the motion of Matter.' Within this, the glass vessel is placed like an inner firmament, and inside this the desired creation may take place. The work of alchemy is not primarily to make gold and silver:

> Its special work is this—To make arcana, and direct these to disease . . . The physician . . . must judge the nature of Medicine according to the stars . . . Since Medicine is worthless save in so far as it is from heaven, it is necessary that it shall be derived from heaven . . . Know, therefore, that it is arcana alone which are strength and virtues. They are, moreover, volatile substances, without bodies; they are a chaos, clear, pellucid, and in the power of a star.[1]

Ordinary herbal brews, said Paracelsus, were unlikely to be of great value since medicine should be of a subtle and potent composition, the original substance having undergone genuine transformation. Man himself has a level of being that corresponds to the celestial; therefore, if he is ill, harmony should be restored at this level rather than at the gross physical level only:

> The third fundamental part, or pillar of true medicine, is Alchemy. Unless the physician be perfectly acquainted with, and experienced in this art, everything that he devotes to the rest of his art will be vain and useless. Nature is so keen and subtle in her operations that she cannot be dealt with except by a sublime and accurate mode of treatment. She brings nothing to the light that is at once perfect in itself, but leaves it to be perfected by man. This method of perfection is called Alchemy. For the Alchemist is a baker, in that he bakes bread; a wine merchant, seeing that he prepares wine; a weaver, because he produces cloths. So, whatever is poured forth from the bosom of Nature, he who adapts it to that purpose for which it is destined is an Alchemist.[2]

Paracelsus, then, saw alchemy as a type of operation that could be perceived in the transformations of Nature, and he taught that the body itself is an alchemist. It transforms food and utilizes the beneficial substances, eliminating the rest. Here again Paracelsus was ahead of his time from the scientific point of view in seeing a relationship between chemistry and biochemistry. And from alchemy, he took the principle that a poison may contain much that is good within it. Poison, he said, is a relative term— 'everything in itself is perfect'; only when the uses of a thing are considered do we then label it poisonous or healthful: 'Remember that God has formed all things perfect, in so far as regards their utility to themselves, but imperfect to others. Herein rests the foundation of the entity of poison.'

Arguing that what could be a poison in its gross form could also be a powerful medicine when prepared correctly, he went against the traditional Galenic view of curing through opposites. The arcanum of a substance could be used to cure the evil effects which the substance itself produced. In homeopathy, minute doses of a substance are given to cure symptoms that correspond to those that the same substance would provoke if the patient had taken it in a larger quantity: Belladonna, for instance, in a homeopathic dilution, may be used to treat delirium and fever—standard symptoms of belladonna poisoning—even though the patient has not in fact taken belladonna in its normal form. Homeopathy also follows the attempt of Paracelsus to work in the subtler realms of matter and mind, since the doses are so diluted that they pass beyond the level of normal measurable chemical dosage and may be said to correspond, broadly speaking, to the Paracelsian 'quintessence' or arcanum of the matter and to affect, accordingly, a deeper level of the patient's metabolism, a level at which psyche and body interact.

Paracelsus shook the complacent foundations of medicine and overthrew the unquestioning reliance on ancient texts and practices. Even his critics could not ignore the success he had with his patients, for he was able to cure cases of gout, leprosy, and epilepsy, which physicians were virtually unable to treat. He was a true individualist who used alchemy in an original and beneficial way.

Science and Alchemy

Alchemy has always maintained a connection with the more practical arts of pharmacy and metallurgy, allowing an interchange of techniques and information. Frequently, processes initiated in the alchemical laboratory have emerged eventually into the everyday world as significant discoveries. A fine example, drawn to our attention by Sherwood Taylor, is that of distillation and the preparation of alcoholic spirits. From about AD 100 until the thirteenth century, distillation was exclusively an alchemical process; pharmacists of the time only used extraction, rather than the chemical technique of vaporizing and condensing. In the early Middle Ages, alchemy went a step further and distilled wine into *aqua ardens*—brandy, a commonplace to us, but a marvel when it was first discovered. It was a manifestation of the alchemical aspiration to combine the two elements of fire and water, for it was both liquid and inflammable. Its medicinal powers were found to be great, providing warmth and recovery from shock. Alcoholic spirits could also preserve other organic materials and be used to extract essential oils from plants.

A list of achievements contributed by alchemy to science is given in *The Morning of the Magicians* by Pauwels and Bergier. They include: the production of potassium lye by Albert le Grand (1193–1280), the discovery of sodium sulphate by Johann Glauber (1604–68), of benzoic acid by Blaise Vigenere (1523–96), the recognition of gases by Johann-Baptiste Van Helmont (1577–1644), and the production of tin monoxide by G. della Porta (1541–1615).

The most potent and fascinating fusion of alchemy and science, however, came in the seventeenth and early eighteenth centuries with the work of eminent scientists such as Robert Boyle and Sir Isaac Newton. Both practised alchemy, both were inspired by its creed, and both claimed to have achieved alchemical results. For these, and other scientists of the period, alchemy and science were bound up together, with alchemy influencing, and being influenced by, mechanical theories of matter, and science itself resting on a basis of mysticism and metaphysics. To the seventeenth-century mind, the worlds of nature, man, and the divinity were inseparately related, and to study one without acknowledging the others was considered to be a distortion of the truth. This was the spirit in which Newton and his contemporaries worked. **Sir Isaac Newton** (1642–1727) was born into a Lincolnshire family. A scholarly uncle took an interest in his education, sending him first to school at Grantham and then to Cambridge, where he eventually became a Fellow of Trinity College. His public reputation was always high: he was made Warden of the Mint in 1696 and knighted in 1705, by which time he was also President of the Royal Society.

Newton is best known now for his formulation of the theory of gravity, his discovery of the spectrum in white light, and his laws of planetary motion. But he was also a mystic and an alchemist, versed in Hermetic teachings, the Qabalah, and Neoplatonism. He was probably in contact with Henry More and Isaac Barrow, who were themselves Neoplatonists and in touch with alchemical circles in London. Newton was a secretive and reserved man, and it is only through his numerous unpublished papers and through scattered contemporary references that we have access to his alchemical thought and practice. He had a well-stocked library of alchemical books and maintained his own laboratory. When a biography of Newton was being prepared after his death, his former assistant, Dr. Humphrey Newton, ventured this reminiscence:

> He very rarely went to bed till *two* or *three* of the clock, sometimes not until *five* or *six,* lying about *four* or *five* hours, especially at spring and fall of the leaf, at which times he used to employ about six weeks in his laboratory, the fire scarcely going out either night or day; he sitting up one night and I another, till he had finished his chemical experiments, in the performances of which he was the most accurate, strict, exact. What his aim might be I was not able to penetrate into, but his pains, his diligence at these set times made me think he aimed at something beyond the reach of human art and industry . . . Nothing extraordinary, as I can remember, happened in making his experiments; which, if there did, he was of so sedate and even temper, that I could not in the least discover it.[3]

(The references here to work in the spring and autumn correspond to the traditional alchemical times for starting the Great Work at the equinoxes.) But Newton *did* claim to have achieved success in making the philosophical mercury:

> I know whereof I write, for I have in the fire manifold glasses with gold and this mercury. They grow in these glasses in the form of a tree, and by a continued circulation the trees are dissolved again with the work into a new mercury. I have such a vessel in the fire with gold thus dissolved, where the gold was visibly not dissolved through a corrosive into atoms, but extrinsically and intrinsically into a mercury as living and mobile as any mercury found in the world. For it makes the gold begin to swell, to be swollen and to putrefy, and also to spring forth into sprouts and branches, changing colours daily, the appearances of which fascinate me everyday.[4]

In other words, Newton was acknowledging current atomic theory of matter but was also stating that matter can be broken down in another way and that transformations can take place that bypass the atomic process of combination.

Several of Newton's contemporaries brought alchemy out into the open and endeavoured to formulate its laws in the context of the new spirit of scientific enquiry. **Samuel Hartlib**, resident in England since 1625, was the focus of a circle of keen experimenters who compared results and discussed metaphysical and scientific theories, trying to find a synthesis and a balance between them. A laboratory was set up in Hartlib's back kitchen, and, in more gracious fashion, the enthusiasts also met at Ragley, the stately home of Lord and Lady Conway, who were keenly interested in such matters.

Robert Boyle (1627-91), who moved away from the old, secretive, esoteric way of working, caused great concern to Newton by his frank and open attitude. Boyle thought that he too had succeeded in making philosophic mercury, and Newton prayed that he would keep silence, for such a secret was 'not to be communicated without immense damage to ye world if there should be any verity in ye Hermetick writers.' Boyle's attitude was very different: '[If] the Elixir be a secret, that we owe wholly to our Maker's revelation, not our own industry, me thinks we should not so much grudge to impart what we did not labour to acquire, since our Saviour's prescription in the like case was this: Freely ye have received, freely give.'[5]

Boyle was later to write *The Sceptical Chymist,* in which he attacked the classical view of matter as consisting of the four elements and substituted the theory that an element was that which could not be broken down into any further substances. Whether he considered that alchemy was still a workable principle on this basis is uncertain. In Newton's case, however, research has shown that his knowledge of alchemy and hermeticism was a direct trigger for his discoveries in the realm of physics (see Betty Dobbs: *The Foundations of Newton's Alchemy,* Cambridge University Press, 1975). Without the study of alchemy and mysticism, Newton could not have made the discoveries that he did; nor did he then consider that such discoveries invalidated the occult basis of science.

Chemistry took over from alchemy the accumulated knowledge of laboratory equipment, of chemical processes such as distillation, sublimation and coagulation, and all the formulas, materials, and techniques that dealt exclusively with the physical properties of matter and identifiable chemical changes. Alchemy had been based upon personal effort, religious devotion, and revelation, whereas the new chemistry took as its criteria experiments that could be repeated and theories that could be considered as proven only when identical results happened under identical conditions. Chemistry took the principle of careful observation from alchemy, but denied that the observer could affect the experiment or be involved in it himself. From the mid-eighteenth century onwards, anyone who tried to mix alchemy and chemistry was courting disaster. The unfortunate James Price, commanded to prove the transmuting powers of a powder which he claimed changed mercury into gold, committed suicide by swallowing prussic acid rather than face the sceptical eyes of the Fellows of the Royal Society.

There is no doubt that alchemy could not be called an objective science, as science was defined in the eighteenth and nineteenth centuries. Yet with contemporary science now undergoing a radical shift of viewpoint, and with our fundamental notions of the realities of time, space, and matter all being revised and gaining—once more—a metaphysical aspect, alchemical concepts may yet provide future science with insights into the nature of the universe.

Alchemy and Literature

The drama of the alchemical process made fine material for literary adaptation. The themes of elemental conflict, death of the body, the triumphal union of the king and queen, and the growth of a precious elixir could serve as a structure for expressions of love, tragedy, and Christian aspiration. On a lighter note, the delusions of the naive alchemist and the trickery of the fraudulent transmuter could provoke satirical comedy, exposing man's weaknesses and capacity for deceit. An example of this has already been quoted from Chaucer (see p. 67); the most famous of all is *The Alchemist* by **Ben Jonson** (1572–1637). However much Jonson may have ridiculed alchemy, though, he knew his subject well and could play with its images and implications in an intricate and subtle fashion, as Charles Nicholl has shown in *The Chemical Theatre*. Moreover, in *Eastward Hoe,* Jonson and his coauthors used alchemical principles to provide a psychological structure for the drama; the characters of Frank Quicksilver, Master Golding, and William Touchstone are defined by the alchemical associations with their names, and the interaction between them provides the basis of the plot. Nicholl says:

> The naming of Quicksilver and Golding is not only a means of defining what they are . . . but of suggesting what will happen to them. It also provides a formula for interaction, for as well as having individual chemical properties, mercury and gold had a specific relationship. By introducing a symbolic framework of chemical process and reaction, the authors of *Eastward Hoe* [Jonson, Marston, and

Chapman] turn the essentially static humour-portrayal into an active participant in the play's unfolding.[6]

It has been said that the essence of drama is conflict, and in alchemy conflict leads to transformation through a sequence of different states. Although most men of learning in the sixteenth and seventeenth centuries would have had some familiarity with the terms and aims of alchemy, and would have used its images simply as ornaments and metaphors in writing, authors of Jonson's stature had to understand its ideas at a deeper level in order to use them as the living core of their work.

There are strong indications that **Shakespeare** used alchemy in a similar fashion, to give form and texture to his dramatic themes in certain plays. Two that have been singled out for contemporary attention are *A Midsummer Night's Dream* and *King Lear*. There is no doubt that Shakespeare was well acquainted with occult traditions;[7] he was well versed in the Christian Qabalah, astrology, magic, and, it seems, alchemy. It must be speculation as to what extent Shakespeare practised any of these subjects, but it is clear that he had enough insight into them to weave them skilfully into his writing.

A Midsummer Night's Dream, for instance, can be interpreted successfully as an alchemical drama, as the Theatre Set-Up company proved in its research and 1983 production. Its conclusion is that Shakespeare used a heady mixture of Celtic lore and alchemy to give the 'Dream' its enchanting quality. Programme notes point to the theme of the four lovers, who to reach true harmony and a proper relationship must first be disrupted and set in conflict with one another, just as the first material must be broken down if it is to be transformed:

The 'subject matter' or 'raw stuff' (often symbolized by a serpent, dragon or toad and called 'earth' or 'lead') was thought to consist of the elements fire, air, water and earth. These appear in the names of the four lovers; fire in 'Helen' (torch of reeds), air in 'Hermia' (female of Hermes—the Greek for Mercury, whose element was air), water in 'Lysander' (from the chemical loosening as in cata*lyst*—hence the liquid vitriol and water), and earth in 'Demetrius' (son of Demeter, earth-goddess), who thus becomes a subject matter of alchemical process. Helen as fire (often symbolized as a dog—hence 'I am your spaniel') is also his soul (symbolized as a dove, which she is called) or *anima* from which he must be separated, while his 'grossness' is purged and his change tested until he can be re-animated, as an improved person, and awaken to a 'golden dawn of concluding harmony.'

There are three sets of weddings in the play: that of Theseus and Hippolyta, the royal pair; that of the two couples just discussed; and then the union of Titania and Oberon, who had become estranged. This too is resonant with an alchemical allegory, and the three levels can be seen as body, soul, and spirit, all of which must complete the perfect change if the alchemical process is to succeed. The union of Titania and Oberon may be interpreted as representing the body, since they live in the world of natural magic and are themselves nature spirits; that of the four lovers as signifying the soul (which in alchemy needs the most careful and complex handling); and that of the royal pair as the spirit. The spirit, or 'sulphur,' requires less transformation than the other two, needing rather to be brought out from obscurity and affirmed. Hippolyta, Queen of the Amazons, has been brought out of her obscurity in that fierce and distant country by Theseus. Even here, a new harmony has to be induced to repair the wounds of battle:

Hippolyta, I woo'd thee with my sword,
And won thy love doeing thee injuries;
But I will wed thee in another key,
With pomp, with triumph, and with revelling.[8]

Puck is the means by which all the trouble is stirred up, causing mischief and misunderstanding by his work: 'The agent of alchemy was Mercury, who "led" the subjects and practised upon them, beginning and finishing the work. This is Puck's function and psychologically he is the "psychopomp" leading the souls, like Virgil in Dante's *Inferno*.'[9] Mercury was depicted as totally volatile, changeable, and elusive, taking the symbolic forms of different beasts, birds, and figures in alchemical illustration. This corresponds precisely to Puck's gleeful speech when he upsets the rustics at their play rehearsal and scatters them into flight in the forest:

I'll follow you, I'll lead you about a round,
Through bog, through bus, through brake, through brier:
Sometimes a horse I'll be, sometime a hound,
A hog, a headless bear, sometimes a fire;

And neigh, and bark, and grunt, and roar, and burn,
Like horse, hound, hog, bear, fire, at every turn.

So through the powers of Mercury, unleashed by the alchemist (in this case perhaps corresponding to Oberon, who is Puck's master), the four elements are set at war with one another and reunited in perfect balance. Titania is humbled and overcomes her pride to become Oberon's consort once more; the three levels of marriage take place and the work is perfected.

In *King Lear*, Charles Nicholl also detects an alchemical theme, with Lear himself as the subject of transformation through his renunciation of power, paternal love, and even his sight. His mortification is complete, and the scene where he is subjected to the elements on the open heath in a dreadful thunderstorm is likened to the stage in alchemy where the matter must undergo violation by fire and water in order to 'die' and be purified.

Blow, winds, and crack your cheeks! rage! blow!
You cataracts and hurricanoes, spout
Till you have drench'd our steeples, drown'd the cocks!
You sulphurous and thought-executing fires,
Vaunt couriers to oak-cleaving thunderbolts,
Singe my white head! And thou, all-shaking thunder,
Strike flat the thick rotundity o' the world!
Crack nature's moulds, all germens spill at once
That make ingrateful man![10]

Lear's own death is the ultimate tragedy, yet through his trials and death, evil has been purged from the kingdom. The concluding 'golden' harmony is not as obvious in *King Lear* as in *A Midsummer Night's Dream*, but alchemical purgation of the gross and exalting of the fine has indeed been seen to take place. Lear's daughter, Cordelia, is like the alchemical material that is despised and mistaken for poison, and yet is the most precious balm of all when it can be seen for what it is. Despatched from the scene early on, she is like the portion of Mercurial water that must be reserved in the alchemical work until it is needed for restoration and nurturing of the injured, mortified matter. Her tears, flowing for her father, are like the alchemical dew that is impregnated with powerful natural force:

All bless'd secrets,

All you unpublish'd virtues of the earth,

Spring with my tears![11]

Later, her kisses are seen as a healing balm:

O my dear father! Restoration, hang

Thy medicine on my lips, and let this kiss

Repair those violent harms that my two sisters

Have in thy reverence made![12]

These are some of the more prominent alchemical parallels to be found in *King Lear*, and readers are recommended to refer to *The Chemical Theatre* for a closer examination of the text and its correspondences with contemporary alchemical material.

A more overt use of alchemical imagery can be found in the poetry of the sixteenth and seventeenth centuries, though in the case of the so-called Metaphysical Poets, this often needs careful deciphering. **John Donne** (1573–1631) frequently utilized alchemical themes in his poetry, either as passing images or as extended metaphors through which to explore the nature of love. In 'A Nocturnall upon S. Lucie's Day' he compares his state to that of the material that has absorbed light and moisture and now lies blackening in the vessel, dying to be reborn as the elixir:

'Tis the yeares midnight, and it is the dayes,

Lucies, who scarce seaven houres herself unmaskes,

The Sunne is spent, and now his flasks

Send forth light squibs, no constant rayes;
    The world's whole sap is sunke:

The general balme th'hydroptique earth hath drunk,

Whither, as to the beds-feet, life is shrunke,

Dead and enterr'd; yet all these seeme to laugh,

Compar'd with mee, who am their Epitaph.

Study me then, you who shall lovers bee

At the next world, that is, at the next Spring:

For I am every dead thing,
    In whom love wrought new Alchimie.
    For his art did expresse

A quintessence even from nothingnesse,

From dull privations, and leane emptinesse

He ruin'd mee, and I am re-begot

Of absence, darknesse, death; things which are not.

George Herbert (1593–1633) and **Andrew Marvell** (1621–78) also used hermetic allusions in their verse, Herbert often in a simple and devout form, Marvell in a more speculative and philosophical vein. Herbert, for instance, begins his poem 'Easter' with the following lines:

Rise, heart; thy Lord is risen. Sing his praise
    Without delays,
Who takes thee by the hand, that thou likewise
    With him may'st rise;
That, as his death calcined thee to dust,
His life may make thee gold, and much more, Just.

One of the finest examples of a religious poem using alchemical symbolism is by Robert Southwell (1561?–95), who in 'The Burning Babe' saw the alchemical furnace as giving birth to Christ:

As I in hoarie Winters night stoode shivering in the snow,

Surpris'd I was with sodaine heate, which made my hart to glow;

And lifting up a fearefull eye, to view what fire was neare,

A pretty Babe all burning bright did in the ayre appeare;

Who scorched with excessive heate, such floods of teares did shed,

As though his floods should quench his flames, which with his
    teares were bred:

Alas (quoth he) but newly borne, in fierie heates I frie,

Yet none approach to warme their harts or feele my fire, but I;

My faultlesse breast the furnace is, the fuell wounding thornes:

Love is the fire, and sighs the smoake, the ashes, shames and
    scornes;

The fewell Justice layeth on, and Mercie blowes the coales,

The metall in this furnace wrought, are mens defiled soules:
For which, as now on fire I am to worke them to their good,
So will I melt into a bath, to wash them in my blood.
With this he vanisht out of sight, and swiftly shrunk away,
And straight I called unto minde, that it was Christmasse day.

THE PHOENIX
ALCHEMY IN THE TWENTIETH CENTURY

The story of alchemy in the twentieth century is a fragmented one. Firstly, there has been a continuation of the practice of traditional alchemy; secondly, an absorption of alchemy into esoteric teachings; thirdly, a reappraisal of alchemy in terms of psychology; and fourthly, an effort to relate alchemy to the frontiers of science. It may well be that in all ages the approaches to alchemy have been diverse, and that it is only with the passage of time that the general pattern of their direction can be seen. Perhaps we tend to gloss over such divergences and forget that people can practise alchemy with radically different aims, values, and theories.

Traditional Alchemy

Although traditional alchemy fell into a decline during the eighteenth and nineteenth centuries, due mainly to the rise of empirical science, it did not die out altogether. In the Islamic culture, especially, it was still practised in the time-honoured fashion. E. J. Holmyard, an expert on Islamic alchemy, relates that he was acquainted with certain twentieth-century practitioners, one of whom was a learned theologian named Abdul-Muhyi (he came to England and carried out his experiments, unsuccessfully it seems, in a blacksmith's forge in Surrey). Muhyi had contacts with alchemical circles: 'One of his last acts,' wrote Holmyard, 'was to write a letter of introduction to an alchemist friend at Fez, the outcome of which was to give the author the privilege of being taken to see a subterranean alchemical laboratory in the old part of the city.' More than this, one surmises, Holmyard was not allowed to divulge.

Since the general opinion in Europe from the eighteenth century onwards was that alchemy was the occupation of lunatics and impostors, those who have carried out alchemical studies in the twentieth century have tended to keep quiet about their activities. Two of the best accounts of modern alchemy are by Armand Barbault and Archibald Cockren, both of whom seem to have come to alchemy from inner promptings, using historical texts for guidance, rather than by learning the discipline directly from a teacher.

Cockren's *Alchemy Rediscovered and Restored* (1940) contains a brief and over-generalized history of alchemy, but of far greater interest is a section in which he recounts his own alchemical experiments and eventual success. He began with the idea that matter contains a vital principle that can either be perfected and used to promote health, or abused and debased (processed foods, he said, have been robbed of the vital principle and are therefore unlikely to nourish us in the proper way). For his alchemical work, he experimented with different metals over many years until he found the right one (unnamed) with which to begin the process of making the philosophical mercury:

> Here, then, I entered upon a new course of experiment, with a metal for experimental purposes with which I had had no previous experience. This metal, after being reduced to its salts and undergoing special preparation and distillation, delivered up the Mercury of the Philosophers, the Aqua Benedicta, the Aqua Celestis, the Water of Paradise. The first intimation I had of this triumph was a violent hissing, jets of vapour pouring from the retort and into the receiver like sharp bursts from a machine-gun, and then a violent explosion, whilst a very potent and subtle odour filled the laboratory and its surroundings. A friend has described this odour as resembling the dewy earth on a June morning, with the hint of growing flowers in the air, the breath of the wind over heather and hill, and the sweet smell of the rain on the parched earth.

Cockren then had to find a way of storing this subtle and volatile gas; he managed to condense it into a 'clear golden-coloured water.' Later, he added this to salts of gold and through distillation of the mixture obtained oil of gold, or potable gold. To obtain the white and the red elixir, further stages were necessary, which involved treating the black metallic residue left after the extraction of the golden water and calcining it. Cockren calls this the 'salt,' to which he added the 'mercury' and the 'sulphur,' these being the white and the red water he had obtained from the golden mercurial water. He mixed the three principles in appropriate quantities, sealed them into a flask, and subjected them to a regulated heat. I quote here from his description of the change in the vessel, since it corresponds very closely with Newton's account (see p. 113): 'On conjunction the mixture takes on the appearance of a leaden mud, which rises slowly like dough until it throws up a crystalline formation rather like a coral plant in growth. The "flowers" of this plant are composed of petals of crystal which are continually changing in colour.' From this point the process goes through the familiar stages of *nigredo,* conjunction, birth of the 'son,' peacock's tail, and finally the white then the red elixir. Cockren was known to his contemporaries as a sincere and intelligent man; in addition he had a first-class professional scientific training, being a specialist in the field of physiotherapy and massage. His chief interest in alchemy was in its medical applications, and he follows Paracelsus in believing that all true medicine must be derived from purified substances, materials that have 'passed by fire to a second birth.' His statement of faith is that:

> I put forward these ideas because I believe that in the medicine of metals there is a perfect curative system; that in the seven metals, gold, silver, iron, copper, tin, mercury, and lead, can be found elements to cure all discords in the human body, and that when this system is properly understood and practised, the multitude of remedies may be discarded. Be it understood that this is not my system, but one which is as old as man himself.

Armand Barbault, a Frenchman, also regarded the greatest good of alchemy as the production of effective medicine. He seems to have been of a very different character from Cockren, however—something of a cult figure, a showman-magician-alchemist as opposed to the retiring and shy disposition of Cockren. His approach to alchemy is more original, and although he claimed to follow the signs and indications given in old texts and illustrations, yet he interpreted them very much in his own way. His account in *Gold of a Thousand Mornings* makes worthwhile reading and brings out some interesting alchemical implications, especially concerning the role of astrology and the power of plants; but taken as a whole it is less convincing and definitely hovering more 'on the edge of the etheric' than Cockren's work.

Barbault worked almost exclusively with organic matter. His Primal Material, which he called the 'Philosopher's Peat,' had to be gathered under correct locational and astrological conditions from about ten centimetres underneath the surface:

> What *is* this First Matter hidden several centimetres under the turf? Is it not—at least as far as the layman is concerned—plain ordinary earth? For the initiated person it is something quite different: it is

living earth, seized from the ground by a very special process belonging to the sphere of High Magic, which allows the adept assigned to the task to gain possession of an entire collection of physical and metaphysical principles.

Barbault spent much time and trouble gathering plants and dew for alchemical processing and for adding to the First Matter. Again, he was always careful that the time of day, the season, and the planetary configurations were favourable so that the sap and the dew would be at maximum potency. This concept is certainly worth further investigation, especially as it is now known that the active ingredients in herbs, for instance, can be extracted in greater quantities if the herbs are gathered at a particular time of day, usually in the early morning. Planetary studies, though still in their infancy, are already beginning to reveal what the astrologers have always known—that the tide of life, cycles in growth, fluctuations in composition of organic entities and minerals, and climatic change are all affected by planetary relationships in the solar system. Barbault had at one time been a fashionable professional astrologer, and he assessed each critical moment in the Great Work in detail, choosing a suitable horoscope for starting each stage of the process. Following the alchemical tradition, he also believed that the practitioner's own chart was of vital importance. His horoscope, he boasted, proclaimed his special aptitude for a spiritualized science! (However, astrologers may like to examine his chart, printed in *Gold of a Thousand Mornings,* which shows Neptune rising, square to the Sun, a configuration associated with a mystical but often woolly-minded approach to life and carrying the danger of self-deception in matters of intuition and occultism.)

Barbault worked with a woman (later to be his wife) who guided him in the preparation of his materials. He used her as a kind of psychic medium; she would receive inner messages indicating what he should do next, and at the same time she would monitor the stage of the proceedings by visualising the energies involved. Here are some extracts from Barbault's account of the stage named 'the acquisition of the germ':

> My companion was at this time in a state of high exaltation. She existed for long periods in a trance-like condition and carried out her functions as guide in the fullest possible manner. It was she who chose the exact location for the acquisition . . . she felt irresistibly attracted to the spot where the evolution of the philosophic germ was taking place. The very next day she ascertained that a change in

the active mass had occurred and that it now formed a sphere. This she saw evolving, growing and changing colour—becoming green—while two currents crossed it. Forseeing danger from outside which could threaten the life of the germ, she traced a large circle round the chosen spot, according to the teaching of magic . . . On the ninth day . . . she witnessed a battle between a lion and fearful beasts which were determined not to abandon the philosophic germ. Then, in the evening, a dream revealed to her a whole spectrum of colours whose source was the sun, concentrated exactly where the germ of our Matter was. She reports that she saw for the space of a minute the most beautiful colours in the world. I believe that at this moment the stone was fertilized.

Barbault eventually perfected his elixir and invited various professionals to test it, including the Weleda laboratories. The 'vegetable gold' apparently had extremely beneficial effects upon a number of patients suffering from different illnesses. He would have liked to have initiated full-scale production, but found that the cost of the operation needed was prohibitive. His conclusion was that his medicine was in a different category altogether from conventional medicine, although it had some connection with homoeopathic preparations: '[I realized] that my liquor of gold was not a specific remedy but a universal additive, able to stimulate the effects of ordinary medicine to a remarkable degree by acting on the entire vital field. My medicine does not, therefore, seek to operate on the same wavelength as official medicine.'

Alchemy and Esoteric Schools

Alchemical teachings were absorbed into a number of twentieth-century esoteric teachings. Some occultists, like Barbault, saw in alchemy a potential magical framework, its ceremonial approach and vivid mythological imagery lending itself to the development of psychic abilities and the harnessing of subtle energies. Magic can be briefly defined as the process of learning to understand, manipulate, and interpret energies that exist in ourselves and in the natural world. Most students of magical traditions would agree that magic itself is 'natural' but involves working at a higher level of awareness and sensitivity than normal; it involves great personal responsibility and unless it is practised with proper motivation and discrimination can become tainted with greed or delusions. In these broad terms, alchemy has a great affinity with magic in its emphasis upon releasing the active energy from material substances through the dedication and correct outlook of the practitioner.

The Hermetic Order of the Golden Dawn incorporated alchemy into its occult teachings. The Order was founded in 1887, but it was still intensively active in the first two decades of the twentieth century and its influence may be perceived in many esoteric orders today. It is thought to have had Rosicrucian affiliations, but its origins are shrouded in myth and mystery. W. Wynn Westcott, the founder, claimed to have discovered an old manuscript full of strange and marvellous rituals, which led him into contact with a German initiate, one Anna Sprengel, who gave the newborn Order her blessing and guidance. Controversies have raged about the veracity of this ever since. Whatever the truth of the matter, the driving impulse behind the Golden Dawn was powerful enough for it to grow rapidly in numbers, attracting many members and sympathizers from artistic and literary circles. The Order was carefully structured, conducted on a basis of ordered learning programmes for its initiates, who moved up from one 'grade' to another as they mastered various systems and skills. The Qabalah was taught, as was divination—mainly astrology and tarot. Symbols were painted, magical weapons made, robes sewn, and complex rituals learnt by heart. Among its more illustrious members were W. B. Yeats, Algernon Blackwood, A. E. Waite, Florence Farr, and Anna Kingsford, the exponent of mystical Christianity. Its most notorious prodigy was Aleister Crowley, though he did not stay within the fold for long. The Order itself disintegrated after a tempestuous series of internal squabbles.

Those who wished to proceed through the Order's grades were expected to be familiar with alchemical symbolism and perhaps to have some experience of practical alchemy. With its emphasis on divination, symbolism, and experience of 'higher planes,' the Golden Dawn concentrated more on the revelations that alchemy could bring rather than on its physical process. An instruction, probably written by S. L. MacGregor Mathers, a Chief of the Order, reads as follows:

Before commencing any Alchemical process, and at the different stages of it, bring the Cucurbite, Retort, Crucible, or other vessel containing the Matter, place it in the centre of the table and range the Tablets round it thus: White Tablet with Head (North), Black and Grey Tablet with white pentacle (East), Tablet with Crystal (South), Coloured Tablet with Hexagram (West). (The Operator stands in the South.)

Then endeavour according to the directions to see in the Crystal and go to the Alchemical plane corresponding under the Sephira of (Chokmah) where ask the Governor of Hylech to send down the Divine Light into the Matter, the LVX. Perform what other operations you wish and then remove the Tablets and continue the Alchemical processes as usual. In the intervals between the stages etc., act as here prescribed.

Description of the Plane. A beautiful garden in which is a fountain issuing from a pillar and filling a large oblong basin with a certain white water. This place is guarded by an Angel with a Caducean Wand, who represents Metatron on this plane. Ask him to bring you before the Throne of the Governor of Hylech. Above the Pillar is a Globe and the Bird of Hermes human-headed. Further on is the throne of the Governor of Hylech who has rainbow colours about him. There are also near him the 4 Angels of the Elements, the Red King and White Queen etc. and many other symbolic forms. Ask the Governor of Hylech that the Divine LVX may be sent into the Matter and give as your symbols (the Pyramid) and (the Rose Cross).[1]

Probably the most important contribution that the Golden Dawn made to the alchemical tradition was of perpetuating alchemy itself in an age of scepticism, showing that it could be considered as a system of esoteric knowledge that was an integral part of the Western occult tradition. It also drew out the potential of its symbolism, developing the imaginative powers of its members through active visualization. Without the Golden Dawn, it is quite possible that alchemy would have been quietly pensioned off.

It may also be due to the work of the Golden Dawn that many Western spiritual and occult disciplines today are imbued with some of the symbolism and terminology of alchemy. For instance, following the path of knowledge is often referred to as 'The Great Work,' or simply 'the Work.' Modern descriptions of the Qabalistic Tree of Life, too, draw on alchemical practice. The diagram of the Tree contains at its middle level a relationship between three points—Tiphareth (individuality), Geburah (judgement and strength), and Chesed (love and mercy), and it is often said that this triangular form, with the apex below, is like a vessel in which the soul must be born after a man is purified by being stripped of false values and judgements and becoming receptive to the true quality of love.

G. I. Gurdjieff was a famous Armenian teacher who also presented the basic ideas of alchemy in his 'work,' and used them in an original and inventive form. Gurdjieff was active first in Russia, then in France and America from the early years of the present century until his death in 1949. It is hard to summarize his teachings, which, like those of the Golden Dawn, have had a profound effect upon contemporary esoteric thinking and practice. Perhaps they could be described as 'a science of consciousness,' the teaching of a way through which man can 'wake up' to his possibilities through intentional observation of himself and the world around and through proper direction of personal energies and emotions.

Gurdjieff taught that man possessed several 'centres' of consciousness, ranging from one of powerful instinct to ones of higher intellect and emotion. The body is not to be seen as a separate entity, but is connected to all these centres in specific and often subtle ways—the body is dense matter, whereas spirit is also matter, although very rarefied. He demonstrated that the body is a kind of factory that will convert the food that comes in to nourish itself. However, he did not restrict this to the notion of physical food, but taught that we take in three kinds of food—physical nourishment, air, and impressions. We need all of these to stay alive. (Subsequent psychological experiment has proved Gurdjieff to be right on this score, for a person deteriorates rapidly when placed in an environment with no sensory impressions.) This Gurdjieff described as our own alchemy, the process by which we sift out the different elements from the food, air, and impressions and convert them into a form in which we can digest, store, or use them in our physical, mental, and emotional lives: 'This is our inner alchemy, the transmutation of base metals into precious metals. But all this alchemy is inside us, not outside . . . In man's inner alchemy higher substances are distilled out of other, coarser material which otherwise would remain in a coarse state.'[2]

Psychology and Alchemy

Gurdjieff's teachings were in one sense non-specialist in that they covered the whole spectrum of man's existence and experience—art, scientific theory, psychology, and so forth. In the more specialized field of psychology, however, alchemy has found a natural home. With the growing urge to explore human instincts and mental processes, it became apparent that the alchemical process could be seen as a description of inner transformation. While C. G. Jung (1875–1961), the Swiss psychologist, is the most famous interpreter of alchemy in this light, he was preceded by Major-

General **E. A. Hitchcock** (1798–1870), an American, who scorned the idea that the transmutation of metals was the true aim of alchemy, holding instead that 'man was the subject of Alchemy; and that the *object* of the art was the perfection, or at least the improvement, of Man!'[3]

Jung had no real interest in the laboratory operations of the alchemists, but he found a profound correspondence between its symbolism and the symbolism that often occurs in dreams, particularly dreams that mark times of crisis or transformation for the dreamer. In some of his patients' dreams, he found an almost precise parallel with images used in old alchemical illustrations, even though the patients concerned had no knowledge of alchemy. His basic theory, which has deeply influenced many psychologists, artists, writers, and thinkers ever since, is that the psyche of each person merges, at its deepest point, with the psyche of mankind as a whole (the 'collective unconscious') and that the human psyche—energy in its essence—crystallizes into various fundamental images, which are beyond pictorial image in themselves ('archetypes') but which may surface in the form of a recognizable image or symbol in the consciousness of individual man, chiefly through the medium of dreams and visions. Jung saw that the alchemical symbols (such as the rose, the eagle, the king and queen, the fighting dragons) were themselves archetypes and that the alchemists had, by means of these symbols, described the development of the human psyche itself from its 'raw' state into one of perfection, or gold.

Jung named this whole process 'individuation,' and in doing so broke away from the prevalent theory that signs of disturbance in the individual were necessarily warnings of abnormality; he maintained, rather, that, like the alchemical process, the process of individual growth was one of conflict, crisis, and change. He discovered that by identifying each stage of the alchemical process clearly, by understanding its archetypes and realizing the variety of forms they could take, he could interpret certain of his patients' dreams as parallels of alchemical stages, and could assess their current state accordingly.

Jung was himself always willing to explore aspects of his own psyche and to be affected by dreams and images. His discovery of alchemy emerged as part of his own personal development:

> Before I discovered alchemy, I had a series of dreams which repeatedly dealt with the same theme. Beside my house stood another, that is to say, another wing or annex, which was strange to me. Each

time I would wonder in my dream why I did not know this house, although it had apparently always been there. Finally came a dream in which I reached the other wing. I discovered there a wonderful library, dating largely from the sixteenth and seventeenth centuries. Large, fat folio volumes, bound in pigskin, stood along the walls. Among them were a number of books embellished with copper engravings of a strange character, and illustrations containing curious symbols such as I had never seen before. At the time I did not know to what they referred; only much later did I recognize them as alchemical symbols. In the dream I was conscious only of the fascination exerted by them and by the entire library.[4]

Only after I had familiarised myself with alchemy did I realise that the unconscious is a *process,* and that the psyche is transformed or developed by the relationship of the ego to the contents of the unconscious. In individual cases that transformation can be read from dreams and fantasies. In collective life it has left its deposit principally in the various religious systems and their changing symbols. Through the study of these collective transformation processes and through understanding of alchemical symbolism I arrived at the central concept of my psychology: *the process of individuation.*[5]

Through his contact with alchemy, Jung transformed his own understanding of Christianity:

One night I awoke and saw, bathed in bright light at the foot of my bed, the figure of Christ on the Cross. It was not quite life-size, but extremely distinct and I saw that this body was made of greenish gold. The vision was marvellously beautiful, and yet I was profoundly shaken by it . . . [It] came to me as if to point out that I had overlooked something in my reflections: the analogy of Christ with the *aurum non vulgi* and the *viriditas* of the alchemists . . .The green gold is the living quality which the alchemists saw not only in man but also in organic nature. It is an expression of the life-spirit, the *anima mundi* or *filius macrocosmi,* the *Anthropos* who animates the whole cosmos. This spirit has poured himself into everything, even into inorganic matter; he is present in metal and stone. My vision was thus a union of the Christ-image with his analogue in matter, the *filius macrocosmi.*[6]

In Jung we have an example of a man whose life and work were totally transformed by contact with the alchemical tradition. He could be called an alchemist of the psyche, the guiding Mercurius spirit who could lead men and women through the dangers and trials of the inner process of transformation.

Science and Alchemy, or 'Parachemistry'

Alchemy has now gained a respectable place in the world of psychology and an enduring life in the realms of esoteric teaching. But if it is still to have a physical application as well, then it must reestablish a relationship with modern science and define its level of operation. This is not to say that alchemy is exactly the same kind of discipline as physics and chemistry; but now that modern scientific philosophy is yielding to a more flexible and expansive understanding of the relationship between energy, matter, and consciousness, it may be possible for alchemy to explain its principles of transformation in terms of these three forces and in a way that will be understood by contemporary science.

Fritjof Capra, author of *The Tao of Physics,* argues that the way is now open for a reconciliation between mystical and scientific traditions. The parallels have always been there, but until recently they have been ignored due to the scientist's concentration on what is 'external' and quantifiable, and the mystic's contemplation of reality through inner consciousness. It is ironic that Isaac Newton, mystic and alchemist, should have been the father of deterministic physics, which postulated that through understanding universal laws correctly, all physical results could be correctly predicted from knowledge of present conditions, and that the observer could detach himself completely from the phenomena he was observing in order to assess these conditions and make his predictions. This approach still permeates popular thought and culture, but in fact the pioneers of science have long since moved on from this position to the theory of relativity and the atomic, quantum, and nuclear models of physics. These have brought back the central idea that the observer cannot be detached from what he is observing. Space and time, said Einstein, are interdependent and our experience of events is modified by our relative position and velocity in space. Next, quantum theory showed that the very act of observing subatomic particles will affect the life of these particles; moreover, such particles cannot be defined as energy or matter but can manifest as either, leaving the old distinction between force and matter stranded high and dry. Added to this is the discovery that such 'quanta'— the so-called 'packets' of energy/matter—obey a law of *uncertainty.* Their movement and form can only be predicted as a probability, not because scientists do not understand the laws operating, but because the very law governing them is one of probability rather than certainty. Quantum theory thus comes close to the tenets of alchemy, where it has always been affirmed that there are no guaranteed results even if the alchemist follows the process according to the correct principles. It also reinstates the alchemical principle that the experimenter and the experiment are one, that they mutually affect one another, and that both are bound up within the currents of Nature:

> Quantum theory thus reveals a basic oneness of the universe. It shows that we cannot decompose the world into independently existing smallest units. As we penetrate into matter, nature does not show us any isolated 'basic building blocks' but rather appears as a complicated web of relations between the various parts of the whole. These relations always include the observer in an essential way. The human observer constitutes the final link in the chain of observational processes, and the properties of any atomic objects can only be understood in terms of the object's interaction with the observer. This means that the classical ideal of an objective description of nature is no longer valid . . . In atomic physics, we can never speak about nature without, at the same time, speaking about ourselves.[7]

Capra also points out that some scientists have called for the abolition of the term 'observer' and its replacement with the word 'participator'. There is no neatly packaged way in which alchemy can fit precisely into the new physics, but it can be seen that here, for the first time since the seventeenth century, we have a framework that is potentially large enough to include both.

Some twentieth-century alchemists have attempted to 'explain' alchemy in terms of nuclear theories, just as Jung 'explained' it in terms of the psyche and the Christian spirit.

Both approaches can be valid and fruitful, but should not be considered as absolute. In *The Morning of the Magicians,* Jaques Bergier relates his account of a meeting with a 'mysterious personage,' an impressive and practising alchemist who warned him of the dangers of nuclear science, which was then, in 1937, in a critically expansive phase. He told Bergier that such experiments were fraught with dangers through explosive release of atomic energy and poisoning through radiation. His most startling pronouncement was that the alchemists themselves were in possession of this secret and had used the nuclear principle in their work for centuries—aeons, perhaps—but had done so from 'moral and religious' motivations, which had enabled them to handle the power in a responsible way. Bergier, who had been longing to meet a genuine alchemist, asked the stranger to instruct him as to the true nature of the art:

> You ask me to summarize for you in four minutes four thousand years of philosophy and the efforts of a life-time. Furthermore, you ask me to translate into ordinary language concepts for which such a language is not intended. All the same, I can tell you this much: you are aware that in the official science of today the role of the observer becomes more and more important. Relativity, the principle of indeterminacy, shows the extent to which the observer today intervenes in all these phenomena. The secret of alchemy is this: there is a way of manipulating matter and energy so as to produce what modern scientists call 'a field of force.' This field acts on the observer and puts him in a privileged position *vis-a-vis* the Universe. From this position he has access to the realities which are ordinarily hidden from us by time and space, matter and energy. This is what we call 'The Great Work.'[8]

He went on to state that the transmutation of gold is only a particular application of alchemy, not the goal in itself.

It may well be that alchemy knows another way of altering atomic structure without the use of huge and costly nuclear reactors, and possibly there are clues to this knowledge in the insistence on the almost endless repetition of certain parts of the process, such as distilling and re-distilling the liquid matter hundreds of times.

Although the currently accepted theory is that the transmutation of elements must be achieved by alteration of the composition of the atoms in the element, and that this can be done only through nuclear science, some slight evidence has already been offered to show that this may not always be so. Louis Kevran and other eminent biologists have shown that plants alter the proportion of elements within their composition through some form of transmutation. For instance, oats germinated in a medium containing no calcium were found to have increased their calcium content by more than 100 percent. In terms of modern nuclear understanding, this would seem to be impossible, implying that our understanding of the principles of elemental formation may need drastic revision. Perhaps the old alchemical theories that gold is 'grown' in the earth may have a seed of truth that could be reformulated in the light of modern knowledge.

Alchemy will find it difficult to 'prove' its validity in acceptable 'scientific' terms, however, until the general scope of scientific experimentation and the classification of results are expanded. This problem is not unique to alchemy. Most disciplines that claim a relationship between physical coordinates and the human psyche or higher energies have the same difficulty—including astrology and certain 'fringe' medicines. A common factor in these practices is that each case is treated as unique. The alchemist and his work are one unique phenomenon—no one else can step into his laboratory and take over the work. The horoscope is (to all intents and purposes) unique for the individual concerned, being a map of the relationship of the solar system drawn precisely for the time and place of birth. Each patient, in 'holistic' medicine, is an individual case who cannot be treated exactly the same as another. All these disciplines rest on well-founded principles and techniques that lay down fundamental modes of operation; but all are adapted and varied according to the exact conditions that present themselves to the practitioner. In alchemy, judgement of how and when to proceed must be tempered by one's own inner state, by the physical materials and equipment available, and by the 'celestial climate' as defined by the planetary influences; if all these are not consciously taken into account, and a harmony between them sought, then the work becomes sterile and mechanical.

There are signs that alchemy is due for a revival, practised in a way that is complementary with the expanded view of science but yet maintaining personal responsibility and a spiritual dimension. The Paracelsus Research Society in the United States endeavours to instruct its students in alchemy, with the discipline of conducting organized and recorded research and the aim of producing medicines on hermetic principles. The current level of interest in alchemy is reflected by the fact that over 300 people met at the International Alchemical Symposium in 1980, a conference which included papers on the relevance of alchemy to medicine, astrology, and psychology. In the UK, readers of *The Hermetic Journal* have been invited to try their hand at practical alchemy, starting with very simple chemical experiments performed with complete attention and observation: 'We, as alchemists, must learn to truly experience substance, to see the different ways in which different types of matter and processes within this matter behave, and in this way to approach the essence of substance.'[9]

In our modern world, specialization has become predominant, and the expert is automatically assumed to be someone who has developed skills within a closely defined field of study. Indeed, the range of information and data available today is so vast that no one person could hope to encompass it all. Even in subjects that are apparently related, such as astrophysics and astronomy, specialists in the one usually have little knowledge of the advances being made in the other. Alchemy brings back the hope that it is possible for the non-specialist to grasp the principles upon which the natural world operates, and to apply them effectively. By using the faculties of observation and intelligence, and through the exercise of patience and personal integrity, it is considered, in the hermetic tradition, that real knowledge can be gained, as opposed to secondhand opinions taken from books or teachers. According to the tradition, this knowledge can then be applied in the external world in line with one's personal skills and inclinations. Alchemy affirms that man is not helpless or swept along by a current of 'progress' that he cannot understand or contribute to. It carries the message that man, the image of God, is equipped to seek and to find the secrets of the world through his own personal efforts.

REFERENCES

Abbreviations: HM = *The Hermetic Museum,* ed. A. E. Waite (1893)
                   TCB = *Theatrum Chemicum Britannicum,*
                       Elias Ashmole (1652)

Chapter 1:

1 *The Sophic Hydrolith* (HM).

2 *The Golden Tripod* (HM).

3 Ibid.

4 Cockren, *Alchemy Rediscovered and Restored,* p. 138.

5 *The Book of Lambspring* (HM).

6 *The Sophie Hydrolith* (HM).

Chapter 2:

1 Sutherland, *Gold.*

2 F. Sherwood Taylor, *The Alchemists,* p. 25.

3 Quoted in F. Sherwood Taylor, ibid., p. 24-5.

4 Quoted in Lindsay, *The Origins of Alchemy.*

5 For a discussion of what this and other alchemical apparatus of the early period looked like, see F. Sherwood Taylor, *The Alchemists,* Chapter 4.

6 Michael Sendivogius, *The New Chemical Light* (HM).

7 H. J. Shepperd, 'Alchemy: Origin or Origins?', *Ambix,* vol. XVII (July 1970).

8 Ko Hung (*c.* AD 300) quoted in Needham, *Science and Civilisation in China.*

9 Lao Tsu, *Tao Te Ching,* tr. Gia-Fu Feng and Jane English (Wildwood House, 1973).

Chapter 3:

1 Thomas Norton, *The Ordinall of Alchimy* (1477); first published in English in 1652 (TCB).

2 A. M. Taylor, *Imagination and the Growth of Science.*

3 J. A. West and J. G. Toonder, *The Case for Astrology* (Macdonald, 1970), p. 35.

4 Cornelius Agrippa, *Of Occult Philosophy,* p. 511.

5 Quoted by Lindsay, *The Origins of Alchemy.*

6 *The Golden Tract* (HM).

Chapter 4:

1 Holmyard, *Alchemy,* p. 87.

2 See *The Hermetic Journal,* no. 15 *(Hermetic Note Concerning the Emerald Tablet),* p. 35.

3 See ibid., p. 35; from Julius Ruska, *Tabula Smaragdina* (Heidelberg, 1926).

4 From the *Corpus Hermeticum,* quoted by Lindsay, *The Origins of Alchemy.*

5 Norton, *The Ordinall of Alchimy* (1477, 1652).

6 Ashmole, Preface to TCB.

7 From Allen, *A Christian Rosenkreutz Anthology.*

8 From *Gloria Mundi* (1526), quoted by Read, *Prelude to Chemistry.*

9 *The Sophic Hydrolith* (HM).

10 Translated from Berthelot, *Collection des Anciens Alchimistes Grecs.*

11 HM.

12 Daniel Stolcius, *The Pleasure Garden of Chemistry,* pp. 529, 530, 532, 533.

13 *The Book of Lambspring* (HM).

14 Stolcius, *The Pleasure Garden of Chemistry.*

15 See Paul Baines, 'Dew and Dew Ponds,' *The Hermetic Journal,* no. 17, p. 12.

16 *The Kabbalah Unveiled,* tr. S. L. MacGregor Mathers (Routledge & Kegan Paul, 1970), p. 116.

17 See Adam McLean, 'The Birds in Alchemy,' *The Hermetic Journal,* no. 5, p. 15.

18 John A. Mehung, *A Demonstration of Nature* (HM).

19 *The Golden Tripod* (HM).

Chapter 5:

1 Sir George Ripley, *The Compound of Alchemy* (TCB).

2 In TCB.

3 *The Hermetic Journal,* no. 12 (Adam McLean, *Muller's Process),* p. 27.

4 The full story of Sendivogius and Seton may be read in Holmyard, *Alchemy*, pp. 231-6; see also Rafal T. Prinke, 'Michael Sendivogius—Adept or Imposter?,' *The Hermetic Journal,* no. 15, p. 17, and Stanton J. Linden, 'Jonson and Sendivogius,' *Ambix* (1977-8).

5 Barbault, *Gold of a Thousand Mornings,* p. 51-2.

6 Quoted in F. Sherwood Taylor, *The Alchemists,* p. 67.

7 Flamel, *Explanation of the Hieroglyphicall Figures.*

8 Wei Po-yang (second century AD), quoted by C. G. Jung, *Alchemical Studies.*

9 *The Treatises of Philalethes* (HM).

10 Michael Sendivogius, *The New Chemical Light* (HM).

11 Pseudo-Geber, *The Sum of Perfection.*

12 TCB.

13 Ripley, *The Compound of Alchemy.*

14 Quoted by Holmyard, *Alchemy,* p. 37.

Chapter 6:

1 Heinrich Nolle, *The Chemist's Key,* translation from the German attributed to Henry Vaughan (1657).

2 *The Secret of the Golden Flower,* tr. Wilhelm.

3 Frontispiece to *Musaeum Hermeticum* (1625).

4 Basilius Valentinus, *The Practica* (HM).

5 Michael Sendivogius, *The New Chemical Light* (HM).

6 Flamel, *Explanation of the Hieroglyphicall Figures.*

7 Quoted in *The Hermetic Journal,* no. 14 (Adam McLean, *Jacob Boehme),* p. 23, from the narrative of Manly Palmer Hall.

8 Boehme, *Signatura Rerum* (The Signature of All Things) (James Clarke & Co.), pp. 13, 89.

9 Thomas Vaughan, *The Magical Writings of Thomas Vaughan,* p. 64.

10 Henry Vaughan, 'Cock-crowing.'

11 Yates, *Giordano Bruno and the Hermetic Tradition,* p. 1.

12 *Corpus Hermeticum,* Libellus II, tr. Scott.

13 Ibid., Libellus I.

14 Ibid., Libellus XI.

15 Adam McLean, *The Hermetic Journal,* no. 12 *(Heinrich Khunrath),* p. 35·

16 *The Confession,* p. 132.

17 Quoted in Godwin, *Robert Fludd,* p. 62.

Chapter 7:

1 Paracelsus, *Alchemy, the Third Column of Medicine* (ed. A. E. Waite).

2 Ibid., p. 148.

3 Quoted in Dobbs, *The Foundations of Newton's Alchemy.*

4 Ibid.

5 Ibid., p. 108.

6 Nicholl, *The Chemical Theatre.*

7 See Frances Yates, *The Occult Philosophy in the Elizabethan Age.*

8 *A Midsummer Night's Dream,* I, i.

9 Theatre Set-Up programme notes, 1983.

10 *King Lear,* III, iii.

11 Ibid., IV, iv.

12 Ibid., IV, vii.

Chapter 8:

1 Gilbert, *The Golden Dawn,* pp. 65-6.

2 P. D. Ouspensky, *The Fourth Way* (Routledge & Kegan Paul, 1957), p. 220.

3 Luther H. Martin Jr., 'A History of the Psychological Interpretation of Alchemy,' *Ambix* (March 1975).

4 Jung, *Memories, Dreams, and Reflections.*

5 Ibid.

6 Ibid.

7 Capra, *The Tao of Physics,* p. 71.

8 Pauwels and Bergier, *The Morning of the Magicians,* p. 24.

9 'Working with Practical Alchemy, No. 1,' *The Hermetic Journal,* no. 14, p. 37.

SELECT BIBLIOGRAPHY

Key books for historical study:

Burland, C. A., *The Arts of the Alchemists* (Weidenfeld and Nicolson, 1967).

Holmyard, E. J., *Alchemy* (Pelican, 1957).

Lindsay, Jack, *The Origins of Alchemy in Graeco-Roman Egypt* (Frederick Muller, 1970).

Nicholl, Charles, *The Chemical Theatre* (Routledge & Kegan Paul, 1980).

Read, John, *Prelude to Chemistry* (G. Bell and Sons Ltd., 1936).

Taylor, F. Sherwood, *The Alchemists* (Paladin, 1976).

Collections of alchemical texts and illustrations:

Allen, Paul M., *A Christian Rosenkreutz Anthology* (Rudolf Steiner Publications, 1968).

Ashmole, Elias, *Theatrum Chemicum Britannicum* (1652).

Berthelot, P. E. M., *Collection des Anciens Alchimistes Grecs* (Paris, 1888).

de Rola, Stanislas K., *The Secret Art of Alchemy* (Thames and Hudson, 1973).

Waite, A. E. (ed.), *The Hermetic Museum* (1893); first English translation 1678.

Books of interest on alchemy and related subjects:

Ambix (periodical), ed, F. Sherwood Taylor, London.

Barbault, Armand, *Gold of a Thousand Mornings* (Spearman, 1975).

Boehme, Jacob, *The Signature of All Things (Signatura Rerum)* (James Clarke, 1969).

Capra, Fritjof, *The Tao of Physics* (Wildwood House, 1975).

Cockren Archibald, *Alchemy Rediscovered and Restored* (reprinted by Health Research, California, 1963).

Dobbs, Betty, *The Foundations of Newton's Alchemy* (Cambridge University Press, 1975).

Flamel, Nicolas, *Explanation of the Hieroglyphicall Figures* (1624).

French, Peter, *John Dee* (Routledge & Kegan Paul, 1972).

Geber (Jabir), *Works*, ed. E. J. Holmyard (Dent, 1928).

Gilbert, R. A., *The Golden Dawn: Twilight of the Magicians* (Aquarian Press, 1983).

Godwin, Joscelyn, *Robert Fludd* (Thames and Hudson, 1979).

The Hermetic Journal, edited by Adam McLean (quarterly), Edinburgh.

Hopkins, A. J., *Alchemy: Child of Greek Philosophy* (AMS Press Inc., 1967).

Jung, C. G., *Memories, Dreams, Reflections* (Collins/Routledge & Kegan Paul, 1963).

————, *Psychology and Alchemy* (Routledge & Kegan Paul, 1953).

Needham, Joseph, *Science and Civilisation in China* (Cambridge University Press, 1956).

————, *The Shorter Science and Civilisation in China* (Cambridge University Press, 1978).

Pauwels, L., and Bergier, F., *The Morning of the Magicians* (Avon Books, 1968).

Paracelsus, *Archidoxes of Magic* (Askin, 1975).

————, *Hermetical and Alchemical Writings,* ed. A. E. Waite (1894).

Powell, Neil, *Alchemy: The Ancient Science* (Aldus Books, 1976).

Scott, Walter (tr.), *Corpus Hermeticum* (Dawsons, 1969).

Sutherland, C. H. V., *Gold* (Thames and Hudson, 1959).

Taylor, A. M., *Imagination and the Growth of Science* (John Murray, 1966).

Thorndike, Lynn, *A History of Magic and Experimental Science* (Columbia University Press, 1923-58).

Vaughan, Henry, *The Complete Poems* (Penguin, 1976).

Vaughan, Thomas, *The Magical Writings of Thomas Vaughan,* ed. A. E. Waite (Health Research, California, 1974).

Wilhelm, Richard (tr.), *The Secret of the Golden Flower* (Routledge & Kegan Paul, 1965).

Yates, Frances, *Giordano Bruno and the Hermetic Tradition* (Routledge & Kegan Paul, 1964).

————, *The Rosicrucian Enlightenment* (Routledge & Kegan Paul, 1972).

INDEX

TO OUR READERS